By Night:
Sermons & Meditations
in a Third Millennium

By Night:
Sermons & Meditations in a Third Millennium

The Reverend E. Clifford Cutler
Rector of Saint Paul's Episcopal Church, Philadelphia

Copyright © 2010 by the Reverend E. Clifford Cutler.

Library of Congress Control Number: 2009913842
ISBN: Hardcover   978-1-4500-1685-8
               Softcover   978-1-4500-1684-1
               Ebook   978-1-4500-1686-5

All rights reserved. No part of this book may be reproduced or transmitted in any form or by any means, electronic or mechanical, including photocopying, recording, or by any information storage and retrieval system, without permission in writing from the copyright owner.

The Scripture quotations contained herein are from the New Revised Standard Version Bible, copyright © 1989 by the Division of Christian Education of the National Council of the Churches of Christ in the U.S.A. Used by permission. All rights reserved.

This book was printed in the United States of America.

Cover photograph: Moonrise over the south pasture of the Cutler farm in Bradford, Vermont, by author.

To order additional copies of this book, contact:
Xlibris Corporation
1-888-795-4274
www.Xlibris.com
Orders@Xlibris.com

Contents

Preface xi

Prologue

We Came By Night to Jesus..3

Sermons
9/11 Triptych

"The Night of Racism—Two Days before 9/11" 17
"Darkness came over the whole land; still grace overflowed"...........21
"Rescue dogs, Stewardship and Love"..25

2006

"Stepping Stones"..31
"I Can See the Cross in You"..35
"Larry King Live and a Father's Love"..38
"Violence or Mending: the Forbidden Fruit or the Bread of Life?"........42

2007

"The Workplace is Holy"...47
"Racism and Uprootedness"..50
"Mother Teresa and God's Absence"...54
"God's Dream and the Universal Lie"...58

Quintet on Community at Saint Paul's

"Identity, or the Soul of Saint Paul's"...65
"The Transition Game"..68
"New Directions—Finding the Way Forward".............................71

"Foundational Difference-Making" 75
"Outpouring—Pouring Out Life Cycle" 78

2008

"Overcoming Fear, Seeking Peace" 83
"Eye Openers—Seeing Beyond Difference" 86
"Forgiveness and Singing that will Never Be Done" 89
"Lunar Eclipse, Our Masks and God's Grace" 92

2009

"Transfiguring Vision" 97
"Righteousness is Relationship" 100
"Generativity" 103
"Setting our Sights on the Father of Lights" 106

Global Financial Crisis—triptych

"Wild Fluctuations and Steadfastness" 113
"A hand to grasp, a prayer to give" 116
"Dis-lodged and Graced" 119

Epilogue

Seek the Peace of the City 125

To Amy

~ *"The point is once you've given your heart
there are no replacements."*

May your word be an energizing word, O LORD,
passing from ear to heart, from heart to life:
that as the rain returns not empty, but waters the earth;
so neither may your word return empty,
but accomplish that for which it is given. Amen.

>   —A prayer after George Herbert
>   *George Herbert: The Country Parson, The Temple*; edited, with an Introduction by John N. Wall, Jr.; New York: Paulist Press, 1981; p. 114.

Preface

Time Magazine in November previewed its December 7th issue, 2009, calling the first years of this new millennium the "Decade from Hell." They found neglect, greed, self-interest and deferred responsibility, but not much good news. What follows is a collection of sermons that seeks what is brightly flaring beyond in the night of what *Time* has called this "most dispiriting and disillusioning" decade.[1]

I have bracketed the sermons with two meditations. The first was written at the turn of the millennium and explores the theme of night in works of non-fiction, fiction and poetry (1998) that appeared in the year 1999. Never far from the surface in what follows is the biblical account of Nicodemus' visit to Jesus "by night." The concluding meditation or epilogue explores the night of violence in the city of Philadelphia and in Israel/Palestine with a bright vision of peace-making.

The sermons that follow were not written for publication but to be learned and preached. I sometimes like to think of them as being told. Our second rector at Saint Paul's felt the preacher "should go forth . . . free from manuscript . . . and speak to (people) from a full heart and head that which he thinks will prove God's word in season."[2] The sermons here are picked out of the weekly round of ongoing pastoral care in an Episcopal Church whose vision is to "turn—each to the other—in Christ." Often this happens with a kind of "night vision." There is a lot of mystery to each of us, and it is out of that that we often discover Christ. It takes patience, humility, compassion and hope.

The sermons themselves are arranged in a kind of ascent and descent. They begin with a triptych of sermons preached at Saint Stephen's Church, Cohasset in the Diocese of Massachusetts around the "night" of 9/11. It is striking that in the normal round of preaching a sermon on racism and demonizing others should come two days before the World Trade Center attack. The sermons next pick up at Saint Paul's Church whose vision is described above. I have included four sermons each from 2006 and 2007. The first included for 2006 is the opening sermon at Saint Paul's. The start of a new relationship carries the humility of all that we do not know about each other. It is a kind of darkness in which together Jesus is found. The center or summit of the book contains a quintet of sermons on the nature of parish community—identity, transition, new direction, difference-making and stewardship. The descent again finds four sermons from 2008 and 2009. The opening sermon for 2009 appears 7 and ½ years after the darkness of 9/11 at the death of Beverly Eckert whose husband Sean was killed in the Twin Towers and whose vision for the next seven years of her life was transfiguring. The sermons conclude with another triptych from the darkness of the global financial crisis. Even in that night taken with all seriousness there is a bright morning star to be sought and hoped for.

I wish to thank Robert Busser who encouraged me to compile this collection of sermons and meditations. Bob grew up next door to my grandparents in Germantown, is a member of Saint Paul's where most all the sermons in this book were preached, and whose work took him to my prior congregation where the 9/11 triptych was heard.

"Telling" sermons without notes or text gives an immediacy that is hard to capture with the written word. The 19th century Welsh preacher John Elias cautioned that the preacher "cannot carry fire in paper!" A colleague Matthew Wilkes retorted, "paper will do very well to light the fire with!"[3.] Though I don't see myself as a "barn-burner" of a preacher, perhaps this paper has lit some sparks of love, has fed the constant burn of faith, and banked the coals for tomorrow's fire of hope. The Letter to the Hebrews says of the angels, God "makes his angels winds, and his servants flames of fire" (1: 7). Compiling the words if not the fire here, I have tried as far as is possible to reference illustrations and quotations. Because of lapses in memory or the loss of the reference itself this has not always been possible. As I become aware of omissions I will make the necessary corrections.

November 30, 2009—Saint Andrew, the Apostle

Notes:

1. Serwer, Andy, "The Decade from Hell," in *TIME*, Vol. 174, No. 22, 2009, pp. 30-38.

2. Howe, M. A. DeWolfe; *The Life and Labors of Bishop Hare: Apostle to the Sioux;* New York: Sturgis & Walton Company, 1913; p. 232.

3. Hood, the Rev. Paxton; *Christmas Evans: The Preacher of Wild Wales;* London: Hodder and Stoughton, 1881; p. 187.

John 3: 1-10
Nicodemus Visits Jesus

Now there was a Pharisee named Nicodemus, a leader of the Jews. He came to Jesus by night and said to him, 'Rabbi, we know that you are a teacher who has come from God; for no one can do these signs that you do apart from the presence of God.' Jesus answered him, 'Very truly, I tell you, no one can see the kingdom of God without being born from above.' Nicodemus said to him, 'How can anyone be born after having grown old? Can one enter a second time into the mother's womb and be born?' Jesus answered, 'Very truly, I tell you, no one can enter the kingdom of God without being born of water and Spirit. What is born of the flesh is flesh, and what is born of the Spirit is spirit. Do not be astonished that I said to you, "You must be born from above." The wind blows where it chooses, and you hear the sound of it, but you do not know where it comes from or where it goes. So it is with everyone who is born of the Spirit.' Nicodemus said to him, 'How can these things be?' Jesus answered him, 'Are you a teacher of Israel, and yet you do not understand these things?

Prologue

We Came By Night to Jesus

A Spiritual Reading at the Start of a New Millennium
January 1, 2000

This is a reading taken at the turn of the second millennium the way a nurse might take a reading of vital signs. In this spiritual reading, the instrument I have chosen to use is the imagery of "night." Nicodemus in the Gospel of John came to Jesus by night. I am turning the phrasing around to suggest that in this third millennium it is by night that we come to Jesus. In the one case, in John's Gospel, night carries the meaning of untruth or even evil. Judas, for instance, leaves the last supper, incriminating piece of bread in hand, "And it was night," John adds (John 13: 30). While this meaning of evil-doing still holds, night is also a place of mystery, of exploration and seeking. We come to Jesus by the humility of all that we do not know. In December, 1999 NASA was directing the Mars Polar Lander to touch down on the surface of Mars, probing the unknown of that planet that is a kind of "night" to us. It may be that by our journeying out into such "nights" we will discern the presence of Jesus as "cosmic Christ." The Word goes out from God to use Jürgen Moltmann's phrase in the vibrancies of God's Spirit. "Cosmic vibration is the origin and ground of all forms of energy and matter in the cosmos. The vibrating breath of God is, as it were, the note to which the creation of the world is tuned." [1] Our exploration into the dark of deep space or the neurochemistry of the brain can lead us in the direction of God, the *musicum Carmen,* the musical utterance or vibrancy that is at the heart of all that is.

When the Welsh poet Henry Vaughan wrote of Nicodemus' visit to Jesus by night he observed, "There is in God (some say)/ A deep, but dazzling darkness . . ."[2] To reverse the imagery somewhat we explore the dark, impenetrable mystery and come to Jesus. A contemporary Welsh poet, Gwyneth Lewis wrote an extended poem in 1998 called "Zero

Gravity." She calls it a space requiem in memory of her sister-in-law who died the year before, and to commemorate in the same year the voyage of her cousin Joe Tanner and the crew of the Space Shuttle STS-82 out into the dark of space to repair the Hubble Space Telescope. Though her poem does not mention God, God is present almost as cosmic vibration throughout. And rather than seeing in God a deep, but dazzling darkness, Lewis sees that in the darkness there is something dazzling, flaring "here" and "there" together, taking place beyond—that though she does not name it (it is beyond naming) is God. [3.]

This journey by night toward Jesus at the turn of the millennium is illustrated by three writers, a psychiatrist, a novelist and a poet. I am interested in people who think deeply and in some cases pray deeply about what God is saying to them and what resonates in our world to the rhythms and vibrancies of God. What God is saying to the people of God (what they tell us of their epiphanies) on the threshold of this third millennium is perhaps not so different from what God has uttered before, though in thousands of years the world has changed many times over, almost to be unrecognizable. The role of journey, of human limitation and the need for forgiveness, of entering the night and finding Jesus in whom all things are reconciled and held together, are still all part of what it means to stand on the threshold of the third millennium.

Three Writers at the turn of the Millennium

Psychiatrist Robert Coles

Psychiatrist Robert Coles in a self-effacing tale from his 1999 book *The Secular Mind* relates visiting his friend, novelist, and fellow-psychiatrist Walker Percy. Dr. Percy would go to pray alone in the Covington Church for a few minutes every day while Coles remained outside sitting on the steps. I asked a friend who is an acquaintance of Robert Coles how it is that someone who is as interested as he is in the spiritual is so unable to avail himself of the church community. His suggestion which may or may not be accurate is that Coles "knows that he is fundamentally loved. He is just not sure who it is that is doing the loving. But perhaps knowing you are deeply loved is enough." [4.]

Robert Coles is journeying by night but not intentionally to Jesus. He argues that the exploration of the unknown is one of the principal characteristics of where we are headed as we turn to enter the 21st century. He imagines scientific discovery that will "at last, give us knowing access to our own nature as explorers, discoverers: mind investigating brain . . ." [5.] Whereas the secular has been denigrated by some religious leaders as lacking in moral bearings he sees deep value in the secular mind probing, wondering, reaching, seeking mastery.

The particular exploratory journey that has just opened up is humankind's increasing competence to understand the brain. The brain that has explored the earth and now the galaxy will be able with increasing precision to probe itself. The voyage has become inward. The field of neurochemistry is invested with great hope in this exploration. "Already biochemistry (in the form of lithium and other drugs) has brought manic-depressive illness under some substantial degree of control;" with positive responses from drugs that work against schizophrenia's symptoms, and the anxieties and mood disorders of more "normal" people.[6.] Neuro-biologists are allowing for a biological psychiatry that is increasingly credible and competent.

With what he sees as society's shift away from the sacred, Cole cautions about investing faith in science. "With God gone for so many intellectual pioneers of the last two centuries, the rest of us, as students and readers . . . have only ourselves left as 'objects' of attention."[7.] We imagine a kind of omnipotence, gaining control over vulnerabilities and inadequacies. He warns against the belief that whatever our need there will one day be a pill for it.

There is a place Coles seems to say for limits. One needs a degree of humility before the mystery of creation, transcendent authority, encountering the limits of what one can do. In conversations with Anna Freud the subject of "narcissistic personality" in certain children came up. "These children aren't afraid of being caught, judged, sentenced, and punished by their conscience, their Super-ego; if they are afraid of anything (and some of them seem brazenly fearless!), they are scared that they will be able to do anything, that there are no limits."[8.] Some of these needful limits are shaped by the teachings of religious institutions that would be imparted to parents and children alike. Rather than constraints, these boundaries create a freer, more trustworthy space. Walker Percy addressed limits in terms of modesty: "... we ought to stop, every once in a while, and ask ourselves who we think we are. I'm not just talking 'existentialism' here; I think I'm talking about moral self-examination—as in exactly who do you think you are?! There are times when we get so full of ourselves—we've 'lost all modesty.'"[9] Coles concludes his meditation on the secular mind exploring its own dark recesses, becoming more knowing and competent, tempted perhaps toward mastery or perfect control, with a last word appealing for moral pause, self-examination and limit-setting that give proportion, compassion, and a need for forgiveness to the human person.

Author Sue Miller

At the time that Robert Coles wrote about the secular mind, novelist Sue Miller, in a book entitled *While I Was Gone,* examined the same issues through the medium of story: looking at the brain's ability to probe itself and the importance of belief, along with the reality of limits and the need to be forgiven.

Her novel is about a veterinarian, Jo Becker, who is married to an ordained minister named Daniel. One of the things they learn is that there is a limit to the extent to which each of them can be there for the other. Jo reflects early on: "But of all the compromises marriage requires—and in particular, marriage to a minister—perhaps the most difficult for me has been putting my life and my concerns aside when someone else's life and concerns are occupying Daniel's mind. It isn't just that he's busy when this happens, as an architect might be, or a lawyer or a stockbroker or a professor; it's that he's taken up emotionally too."[10] Circumstances such as a betrayed trust and an unyielding hardness have had to be overcome in the course of the novel and Jo reaches an appreciation of human limitations. She says: "I'm trying to allow for this ordinary distance between us. To let him not want me sometimes. Sometimes not to need him. So that when it comes, I can love it more: the approach, the turning back to what we do want most in each other, what we do need."[11]

Limits also create the space within which pain can be borne. They are supportive. Jean Bennett brings a dog with a spinal injury to Jo. The dog needs to be put down. Jean feels guilty and is not able to bear the pain just yet of ending the life of her husband's pet. Jo sets limits to the amount of adjusting, decision-making, and pain that Jean will have to bear. She suggests the remote possibility that steroids may help. "'So we'll try the steroids,' (Jo) said gently. I didn't really think they would help the dog, but I felt they might help her—or at least give her time to adjust to what had happened." [12.]

Sue Miller also sees journey as characteristic of life today—the inward journey of life's end, the exploration of mind probing the brain. And though, like Coles, she values this exploration she raises insightful questions about the secular mind's pursuits if left to itself. The subject first comes up when the dog that belongs to Eli Mayhew is mercifully put to death. Eli asks if Jo has done many of these. A thousand she supposes. Always with a fear that it might not go well. "But mostly, just a kind of terror of the speed with which it happened once I gave the injection, of how quickly the line between life and death was crossed. I thought of that moment with Arthur (the dog), his utter relaxation into death within seconds, my hands on him as he went over." [13.] The terror is about more than giving up life's attachments. If as Robert Coles observed with God gone we have only ourselves as objects of attention, then the line between life and death that is so easily crossed calls into question our whole existence. Where is our mastery?

Eli is a biochemist about to begin work at Beth Israel Hospital as a research scientist. He and his wife Jean have Jo and Daniel over for dinner. Eli asks Daniel about his belief. The question sets up Eli's proposal of what the journey is about today: the mind probing the brain. Miller shows us the secular mind turned loose without limit or moral pause. Eli asks Daniel:

> 'But belief in what? That's what I wonder. In the *soul?*' Eli's voice gave this italics. He did not, you could tell, believe in the soul.
> 'Among other things. The soul. Yes,' Daniel said. Looking back, I would remember his face then, its clarity, its wholeness.
> 'Aha,' Eli said. He seemed, really delighted .... 'But what if I told you that thought, feeling, personality—even faith—are a matter of neurons firing in specific learned pathways in the brain. That's what the *soul* is. That's all. You can extinguish any of it with a simple knife cut or a blow to the head.'
> 'I'd say that had nothing to do with what I was talking about.'

'But look, what I'm saying is that God is an idea. A human idea. He resides in the particular arrangement of the matter in your brain. Change the matter and presto. God is gone.'

Daniel cleared his throat. He said, 'And what *I'm* saying is that I agree you might be able to eliminate my belief by altering my brain, but that doesn't mean God is gone.'

'But where else does he live but in your brain? Your brain and other brains that have been deliberately structured the same way. You're a smart man, you see that. He's an idea, like the idea of life after death.' His hand circled. He smiled. Or the *virgin birth.*' His smile widened. [14.]

Eli misses the clarity and wholeness of Daniel's face that Jo had seen earlier that seemed all the justification one would need for faith. Instead, Eli pushes Daniel further challenging Daniel to make a convert of him since that is what he supposes Daniel's faith is about.

> . . . 'if that *were* what my faith was about, what I'd say to you is that you're not ripe.' . . . 'There has to be some need, some desire, even, for God. Maybe just some sense of something missing in your life. And I don't think you feel that.' [15.]

Such need does not fit with Eli's self-image of mastery. But Eli, it turns out, does have a need. Eli needs to be forgiven. He tells Jo: "I need a kind of forgiveness from you." She observes if we cannot achieve mastery of ourselves and can admit to limitation then we will all need forgiveness.

> It seems we need someone to know us *as we are*—with all we have done—and forgive us. We need to tell. We need to be whole in someone's sight: know this about me, and yet love me. *Please.* [16.]

Jo continues acknowledging how hard it is to ask another to forgive you this way.

> But it's so much to ask of other people! Too much. Daniel makes it easier on those around him: God is the one he asks to know him as he is, to see him whole and love him still. But for us others it seems there must be a person to redeem us to ourselves. It isn't enough, apparently, to know oneself. To forgive oneself, in secret. [17.]

Sue Miller continues the theme of exploration begun by Robert Coles. But it is almost as though the drive of the secular mind for mastery, as vital as this is, is too much to bear. We need another to know us wholly with love—the vibrancies of God. It is by dark, by night, that we come to Jesus, the embodiment of this love.

Poet Gwyneth Lewis

At her sister-in-law's death, Welsh poet Gwyneth Lewis writes, "But the darkness/ is kind. Dawn will heal with colour/ my grief for your consuming core." [18.] One thinks of the prophecy of Malachi: "But for you who revere my name the sun of righteousness shall rise, with healing in it's wings" (Mal. 4:2).

We are not without limits on our exploration, our voyaging. Lewis never says with the secular mind that we attain mastery. She journeys with a clear sense of modesty. Her cousin's return from the weightlessness of outer space is like rebirth. "This point of view," she says, "is radical, its fruit must be mirth/ at one's own unimportance and now, although/ you're famous, a 'someone', you might want much less./ Your laughter's a longing for weightlessness." [19.] We yearn for the mirth that gives proportion and modesty. We explore, and we are finite. Our journey is not self contained. We need one another. We are not able to protect ourselves against vulnerability. While the space shuttle continues its mission, the family vacations.

> Bored early morning down on Cocoa Beach,
> the kids build castles. I know my history,
> so after they've heaped up their Norman keep
> (with flags of seaweed) I draw Caerphilly's
> concentric fortress. Five-year-old Mary,
> who's bringing us shells as they come to hand,
> announces, surprised: 'I am the boss of me.'
> She has a centre. In our busy sand
> we throw up ramparts, a ring of walls
> which Sarah crenellates. Being self-contained
> can be very stylish—we plan boiling oil!
> But soon we're in trouble with what we've designed.
> So much for our plans to be fortified.
> Our citadel falls to a routine tide. [20.]

NASA's Mars Polar Lander, mentioned at the start of this meditation, has now been quiet for three days. This current voyage into the silent dark of Mars seems to have been lost. There is a place admits Coles for limits in our time of exploration.

Still, it is in the dark that we may come in contact with the sacred. The first time Lewis sees the Hale-Bopp comet:

> . . . The comet's tail
>
> is a searchlight from another point,
> and the point is once you've given your heart
>
> there are no replacements. Oh, your soul,
> if that can escape from its own black hole. [21.]

We are not self-contained. There is another who searches us out. The point from which this searching takes place is the point at which we have given our heart. It is only this heart-giving love (whose source is God) that can satisfy. Though in our hyper-consumptive culture we try most everything else. We take it in like a black hole, yet the hunger remains. In the darkness of space and loss the poet finds solace in the comet. "Hale-Bopp's light/ says something dazzling's taking place beyond, involving moving." And finally, the poem concludes that despite grief, "despite dark matter/ in the heart,/ I'm dazzled. 'Here' and 'there'/ have flared together." [22.] Playing in the pool, "A nonchalant father/ throws Saturn rings. Dive for them now and find everything." [23.] The poem ends with the ordinary and extraordinary unity of all things (a ring toss and the planet Saturn), that can be held together in Christ who goes out to all that is, in the vibrancies of God's Spirit, to use Moltmann's turn of phrase. Remembering that Lewis has a Christian sensibility the word "dive" is full of baptismal resonance and brings us through the darkness of submersion into contact and union with all that is.

Lewis sees the task at the millennium's turn as one of voyaging into the dark—the dark of space, of endings, the dark matter of the heart. It is there we may find ourselves weightless. Here is how Lewis imagines her sister-in-law's death:

On her inward journey
she's traveled beyond

the weight of remembering.
The g-force lifts
from her laboring chest.
Forgetting's a gift

of lightness. She's sped
vast distances
already, she's shed
her many bodies—

cancer, hope, regard,
marriage, forgiving.
Get rid of time
and everything's dancing,

forget straight lines,
all's blown away. [24.]

We make this voyage aware of our mortality, the gravity of life and lift off, of limitation and love without limit, of black holes without and within and the capacity to be dazzled. Finally, it is in the dark that we may discover our kinship in the body of Christ, with that which is beyond and with that which is.

Conclusion

Jürgen Moltmann was given an award in early December, 1999 for his book, *The Coming of God*. As a young man he took a voyage into darkness when in a prison camp British authorities pinned up photographs of Auschwitz. He came face to face with the dark matter in his heart. He felt profound shame. He did not deny its presence, nor did he turn away in fear, but he came by darkness. He had been given a Bible and was moved by the words of Psalm 39: "And now, what is my hope? O Lord, my hope is in you." And, "Hear my prayer, O Lord, and give ear to my cry . . ." He wrote: "I never 'decided for Christ' as is often demanded of us, but I am sure that then and there, in the dark pit of my soul he found me." [25.] In this new century, at this time, celebrating the secular mind and rightly so, we journey by night to Christ who catches us as one might be caught in the beam of a searchlight from another point and the point is heart-giving love for which there is no replacement.

This is how God appears to God's people, the epiphanies they have been given, at the end of the second millennium and the start of the third. Where once Nicodemus would have come to Jesus by night, our voyage today is one of probing the night in which we may discover Jesus. We explore the dark of the brain's recesses and of deep space, even the universe's beginnings. We probe the dark matter of our hearts. It is true that we seek mastery but we do well to have an awareness of our own limits, to have a degree of mirth at our own unimportance, a sense of modesty. Perhaps instead of mastery, it is stewardship that we really mean. We need that ache of something missing, and with all we have done the assurance of forgiveness, to have another see us whole and love us, give their heart to us. Perhaps that is enough—to know we are loved. But if we stay with the journey, even if on the steps *outside* a church, or behind the barbed wire of a prison camp, on a sick bed or a space shuttle, we may in the dark become aware that "something dazzling's taking place beyond." We find ourselves reconciled to all that is, of one race with the unity-that-is-three whose inmost nature is communion. Then we will have come by night to Jesus.

If this is your journey and you have come in off the church house steps, or are considering doing so, you will meet Jesus in the preached word that seeks to probe the night. What follows is a selection of my sermons from the first decade of the third millennium. They include the darkness of 9/11 and a severe recession. Sermons hold the precious oil that fuels God's searchlight of heart-giving love. They are not that oil. On a shelf above the entrance to Saint Paul's Church there are a clay jar and lamp that date from the time of Jesus. They are small, primitive and not what one would call beautiful. They hold the clear oil that illumines the way. I hope that this is what the following sermons may hold for you as we probe together the darkness and mystery of the years ahead.

Notes:

1. Moltmann, Jügen, *The Way of Jesus Christ: Christology in Messianic Dimensions,* HarperSanFrancisco, 1990, p. 289.

2. Vaughan, Henry, *The Oxford Poetry Library: Henry Vaughan,* edited by Louis L. Martz, Oxford: Oxford University Press, 1995, p. 151.

3. Lewis, Gwyneth, *Zero Gravity,* Newcastle upon Tyne: Bloodaxe Books Ltd, 1998, p. 28.

4. From a personal conversation with psychologist, Dr. Max Munro.

5. Coles, Robert, *The Secular Mind,* Princeton: Princeton University Press, 1999, p. 186.

6. *Ibid.* p. 178.

7. *Ibid.* p. 123.

8. *Ibid.* p.119.

9. *Ibid.* p. 129.

10. Miller, Sue, *While I Was Gone,* New York: Alfred A. Knopf, 1999, p. 95.

11. *Ibid.* p. 266.

12. *Ibid.* p. 28.

13. *Ibid.* p. 128.

14. *Ibid.* p. 161.

15. *Ibid.* p. 161.

16. *Ibid.* p. 261.

17. *Ibid.* p. 261.

18. Lewis, Gwyneth, *Zero Gravity,* Newcastle upon Tyne: Bloodaxe Books Ltd, 1998, p. 27.

19. *Ibid.* p. 26.

20. *Ibid.* p. 16.

21. *Ibid.* p. 17.

22. *Ibid.* p. 28.

23. *Ibid.* p. 28.

24. *Ibid.* p. 25.

25. Niebuhr, Gustav, "Religion Journal: Religion Award for Book," in *The New York Times,* Saturday, December 4, 1999, quoting J. Moltmann, p. A12.

Sermons

9/11 Triptych

"The Night of Racism—Two Days before 9/11"

14 Pentecost/September 9, 2001

> "... no longer as a slave but more than a slave, a beloved brother—especially to me but now much more to you, both in the flesh and in the Lord."—Philemon 16

Paul sends a letter to a slave owner about living into a transformed life where others are not labeled or owned but regarded as sister or brother. The issue of slavery is still with us. The U.N. conference on racism in Durban, South Africa has raised the issue. Africans at the conference want to label the slave trade engaged in by the countries of Europe and the United States through the 19th century as a crime against humanity. And so it was, though the critique is refused by the countries who engaged in it. Current practices of slavery in the Sudan do not seem to have garnered as much attention. At the same time Israel and Palestine are engaged in labeling and blaming each other, precipitating Israel's departure from the conference along with our own. While this was on a high boil, we watched as Roman Catholic school children with their parents had to walk through hurled bricks, insults, and even a pipe bomb because their path to school took them through a Protestant neighborhood. One group blames the other for encroaching on it's space, without stopping to listen and to try to understand. Instead, the reaction is violent, depersonalizing the other, labeling, blaming and attempting to do away with the offending party. Paul is writing to a slave owner, whose slave was a nobody, a robber, useless—and he is saying: the cycle of labeling and violence that we do to one another has to stop. Onesimus is a slave. Yes, that is true. Now see him as a person, even more a Christian, even more your own brother. How do we transform life where we are so quick to take offense, to label, and blame, in order to live into a new life of fellowship together?

We find it hard. It all reminded me of a story from one of my mentors. It took place thirty years ago. He was rector of a black congregation in inner-city Philadelphia not far from where later I would be vicar of a white congregation. A boy who had been an acolyte at his church grew up to become a policeman in Washington, D.C. At the age of 25 he was killed while attempting to place a man under arrest. The funeral was attended by over a thousand policemen. It was one of his hardest sermons to prepare but in it he asked, "have we become so depersonalized that we can simply put a label on a man and do away with him? Have we really stopped thinking of policemen as people?"[1.] The story came to mind in light of the week's events: have we really stopped thinking of Irish Catholics as people, or Protestants as people, have we really stopped thinking of Palestinians or Israelis for that matter as people, have we really stopped thinking of Africans or African-Americans or persons of my complexion and background as people, or with Paul as he writes from house arrest in Rome, have we really stopped thinking of slaves as people? We need to be transformed. How do we stop the cycle of blaming, labeling, dehumanizing, and doing away with others? As Christians we have to put Christ first and know the cost of doing that, Jesus says.

Paul's letter to Philemon gives us some clues about being transformed in Christ and letting that change the way we relate to one another. First we have to watch the way we label people—Slave, Black, White, Moslem, Christian, Protestant, Catholic, Jew, Policeman and we all know the pejorative terms we could substitute for any of those categories, and more. When we label people we dehumanize them and it is a short step to doing away with them. This is to choose death, but Joshua in Deuteronomy says: "Choose life." For Paul, Onesimus is no longer a useless slave but a useful brother, transformed from possession to person. It is his way of choosing life. We have to watch the hate language. When Jesus says we need to hate mother and father and even life itself to come to him, he is using an Aramaic manner of speaking that means we need to prefer Christ to all else. When we put Christ first all else falls in place. We have to watch the hate language today. We have to choose life.

We need to listen and tell our story. Paul is writing to Philemon and not accusing him of anything. There is no blame in the letter. He is merely and powerfully telling his story. The story is basically this. Onesimus either stole something of value from his master Philemon or else he caused him considerable damage. Onesimus ran away seeking freedom but he did not find it in the dark alley ways of Rome which were a magnet for fugitives and thieves. Lost in every way Onesimus sought out Paul and there discovered that true freedom could only be found in Christ. This is Paul's story and he asks Philemon to receive Onesimus back and listen to his story. It is a story of transformation. Paul asks Philemon to be transformed as well, to listen, to hear the hurt, the hopes, the needs, the joys of the other. Sometimes what we hear is hard to listen to. And we would like to walk out. We refuse to hear the prophetic critique when there may be something in it from which we may grow. To tell our own story and to listen are roads to transformation.

The final thing that both Paul and Jesus say is that we have to say farewell to our possessions in order to live into the promise of God. Philemon has to give up Onesimus as a useless slave to receive him as a useful brother. He has to say farewell to his old self, his old identity as victimized by Onesimus, his old feeling that someone owes him something, in order to live into a new self that is free. Jesus says, "None of you can become my disciple if you do not give up all your possessions." The Greek word for "give up" means to say "farewell." We usually say farewell to people. So when Jesus says to give up all our possessions he means to say farewell to the old self where possessions are everything. Be transformed to where Christ is all. Is it Protestant concern for Catholics encroaching on their space? Give it up. Say farewell to the old self where possessing space is everything. Be transformed to where Christ is all and the other is sister and brother.

Paul writes to Philemon and asks him to receive back the slave who hurt then fled from him. No labeling, no depersonalization, no blaming; Philemon need only listen to his story, try to understand, and discover a person, a child of God, a brother. In Ireland, in Israel, in Palestine, in South Africa, in the Sudan, in the United States, Jesus calls for transformation. Say farewell to the old life of possessing privilege that is unworthy of us. Do not depersonalize but personalize another by listening to their story. Choose life, welcome the other, carry the cross, and live into the new. Impossible, you say? Conflict and the old ways are too entrenched? Yes, probably if it were only up to us. But like Joshua we have set before us a promised land not of our making but of God's giving. Choose, he says. Choose life.

Amen.

Notes:

1. Washington, Paul M., with David McI. Gracie, *"Other Sheep I Have:" The Autobiography of Father Paul M. Washington,* Philadelphia: Temple University Press, 1994; p. 145.

Deuteronomy 30: 15-20
Philemon 1-20
Luke 14: 25-33

"Darkness came over the whole land; still grace overflowed"

15 Pentecost/September 16, 2001

"and the grace of our Lord overflowed for me with the faith and love that are in Christ Jesus."—1Timothy 1: 14

When the planes hijacked by terrorists slammed into the World Trade Center and Pentagon on Tuesday the words that came to me were those of Matthew's Gospel describing Jesus' death—"darkness came over the whole land . . ." The plumes of smoke and flame; the clouds of dust; expressions of horror and care. "Darkness came over the whole land." All of us have been affected by this terror that began in Boston. We know people who died or know people who know people. And darkness has come over the whole land. Matthew is describing such loss and helplessness, that our only recourse is to turn to God. On the day of resurrection, on the first day of the week, today, the Lord's day, death was seen to have been overcome by life, loss overcome by compassion, arrogance was overcome by faith, violence by love. Life is changed not ended we say at the time of death. God's love that surrounds us is eternal and will never let us go. We are held forever in the fellowship of the Holy Spirit. That is our hope. It is what Paul was convinced of.

Paul's experience pictured in the First Epistle to Timothy was that "the grace of our Lord overflowed for me with the faith and love that are in Christ Jesus." When we admit our humanness (Paul described himself as the least of the apostles) and turn to our Creator, our Savior, our strengthening Guide we find the overflowing, inexhaustible grace of God. In our loss and emptiness when we have no power to help ourselves and turn to God: the grace of our Lord overflows for us. In our anger that focuses us and energizes us but risks consuming us, the grace of our Lord overflows for us.

In our horror, the grace of our Lord overflows for us. In our sadness, the grace of our Lord overflows for us. In our inability to forgive when all we can do is turn to God, the grace of our Lord overflows for us. In the need to affix blame deriding others of different races and creeds, we need to let go and turn to God, and the grace of our Lord overflows for us. Where we would go astray or are seemingly unable to take another step, our energy and guidance for life comes from the overflowing grace of God.

Jesus teaches what this grace looks like. He is talking to scribes and Pharisees who in the society of their day had power, and he says God is like a shepherd or a woman who in that day had little to no power. I suppose it is similar to saying God is like a fireman or policeman who risks all to find the lost in a burning and collapsing tower. The lost are precious to God. God seeks out the lost unconditionally. All the lost, those who died, those who are injured, those who are aggrieved, those who mourn, you and me, are found by God whose love will not let one go without searching and finding and rejoicing.

Jesus taught that God was unlike the powerful of his day with their criteria of who is in and who is out, with their command and control of others. God did not will the horror on Tuesday. God does not will untimely death and evil. I do not even think that God stands by and lets it happen. Instead, God confronts and overcomes evil by compassion, and suffering, and life. We do well not to mistake that for weakness. Crucifixion marked the beginning and ending of Jesus' life. In the year of his birth Rome crucified perhaps as many as two thousand rebels outside the wall of Jerusalem.[1] What has changed the world was certainly not that horror but Jesus' compassion that was stronger than death. It is compassion that searches out the lost and is a grace that overflows with faith and love.

God's grace overflows into a fellowship of faith and love. Fellowship is the opposite of the fear and isolation that terrorism breeds. Fellowship is our response to God's grace. It begins for us at baptism which is why I am glad we are baptizing Alexander this morning. I don't know anything more important for us at this time than our fellowship with God and one another.

Fellowship is expressed with faith. Faith is our trust in God. It is the opposite of that arrogance that imagines we can take matters into our own hands. When Moses delayed, the Hebrew people took over, and turned aside from God to worship idols. They created an image in gold of a calf as though that could substitute for God. Arrogance destroys fellowship. When we substitute hatred for God we destroy fellowship. I think a lot of the fear that pervades the current atmosphere is bred by this arrogance. There is no substitute for God. We need the faith that brings us into fellowship with God and one another.

Fellowship is also expressed in love. Paul in 1st Timothy is pictured as a man of violence for whom grace overflowed. Under the impact of God his life moved from violence to compassion. As Paul once labeled followers of Christ as the enemy, we today are to resist the violence that labels Moslems as the enemy. We learned in a course taught here last year by John Gallop [2] that Islam is a faith that reveres the sacredness of all life and enjoins kindliness and cooperation for good. Passions for violence must be turned toward love.

I have heard from so many of you how precious family and friends are in light of the horrid loss on Tuesday. What has become so clear is how important loved ones are. Many whose loved ones are far away just needed to call and hear their voice. Many needed to hug the ones who were close. All said the really important things in this life we are given are the ones we love. Fellowship is expressed in love.

Some time ago a young mother was telling of her grandmother's death. Unlike the deaths on Tuesday this one was expected. But it got her to thinking that the more we lose those who are close to us the more exposed we are to life's dangers. She felt vulnerable. But then as she held her young daughter she thought we have the opportunity in various ways to create our own fellowship. She felt a strange joy out of all proportion to the moment. It was as though grace overflowed for her with faith and love. When we lose those about us we are diminished there is no question. But there is broader ground at our feet where in communion with others we find belonging. And in God there is an openness where all are found and embraced in a love from which not one of us can ever be lost.

This has been a sorrowful week when the country has been exposed to dangers that for most were unimaginable. We as a people have lost loved ones. We lost rescuers when they went in harm's way to save others. Theirs was and is a sacred calling. They followed the Almighty whose outstretched hand has not lost one. To God we turn when in our loss we feel more exposed and vulnerable than before. To God the lost are always precious. In God we can set our feet on the solid ground of faith where grace overflows out of all proportion. There compassion is stronger than death, faith is mightier than arrogance, and love is more enduring than violence. God like a shepherd seeks us out to bring us home to a sheepfold where there is rest "with the saints, where sorrow and pain are no more, neither sighing, but life everlasting."

Amen.

Notes:

1. Carroll, James, *Constantine's Sword: The Church and the Jews, A History;* Boston: Houghton Mifflin Company, 2001, p. 83.

2. The Rev. John Morton Gallop was retired, having been rector of St. John the Evangelist Church in Hingham, MA. He taught a course on Islam at St. Stephen's Church, Cohasset, MA in 2000. He died on June 8, 2005.

Exodus 32: 1, 7-14
1 Timothy 1: 12-17
Luke 15: 1-10

"Rescue dogs, Stewardship and Love"

All Saints' Sunday/November 4, 2001

Love "bears all things, believes all things, hopes all things, endures all things."
—1 Corinthians 13: 7

I had the opportunity last week to hear Jane Goodall speak. [1] She has undertaken the longest continuous field study of animals, in her case chimpanzees, in their natural habitat, and established the Gombe Stream Research Centre in Tanzania. She was in New York City on September 11th. In her talk she reflected on that from the standpoint of her science but also as a person of faith. She contrasted the self-destruction of terrorism with the self-sacrifice of Christ on Calvary. The one was an act of evil, the other of redemptive love. In addition to the firefighters and police, she mentioned the heroism of the rescue dogs who showed signs of depression when they could not find anyone to save. She talked of how alike we are, that all life on earth is deeply related, and that we as human beings have not been very good stewards.

She is using the word stewardship in the same way I have been these past weeks. Last week I spoke of the stewardship of money not in terms of power but of relationship. Stewardship puts us in relationship with all creation. Stewardship is about self-sacrifice not self-destruction. It is about what I can give for the sake of the whole. It is that redemptive love that binds all things together. As such there is nothing arrogant about it. What does Paul say? Love is not arrogant or rude. It does not insist on its own way. Rather it bears all things, believes all things, hopes all things, endures all things. Love never ends, Paul says. Rather than arrogance there is a modesty to stewardship. As we heard in the first reading today, not all of us will make a name for ourselves that will forever be remembered. But the steward gives out of a robust love that never ends. Unfortunately, as Jane Goodall observed we humans have not been very good stewards.

Attention this week at least since Tuesday has been focused on the Middle East. Our bishops stood in protest with Palestinians in front of the Israeli Consulate. There is such a chasm of mistrust between Israelis and Palestinians that it is almost impossible to say anything about the conditions there without stirring a sharp reaction. If stewardship is about relationship then as human beings we have not been very good stewards there. I was in Israel and on the West Bank in 1996 during the Moslem holy season of Ramadan. It was also the end of the 40 day mourning period for the Palestinian terrorist bomber named Ayyash, also known as the Engineer, who had been killed. I rode public buses outside of Tel Aviv. Some months after returning home one of them exploded. This is closer than I wanted to come to terrorism. It is no stewardship. On the same pilgrimage to Palestine I was at the Shepherds' Fields where at Jesus' birth angels appeared to shepherds abiding in the fields, keeping watch over their flock by night. There, Israel had taken land from the village of Beit Sahour which is over 82% Palestinian Christian in order to build a new settlement called Har Homa for 30,000 settlers. Just two weeks ago four new settlements were approved in Palestinian territory. This is no stewardship. I also saw a typewriter man earning a living on the obstacles that are posed to Palestinians who want work. They must stand in line for building and work permit forms that have to be filled out in duplicate by typewriter which few Palestinian households possess. They then get in line for the typewriter man to fill out the forms. Then it is back to the first line in order to get their permit. Permits are issued to adults thirty years or older leaving all the twenty-somethings without work or experience. This is no stewardship.

What impresses me most concerning the current stir about Israel/Palestine after the bishops' demonstration is that nowhere in the press have I heard the mention of nonviolence. The reactions are all about the violence of one group whether Israeli or Palestinian against the other. Stewardship calls us to take another path. On September 11th I wrote: "In stark contrast to this morning's terrorism, a Palestinian Anglican priest commented recently, 'there is now a new intention of trying to intensify a movement of nonviolence. This is the way Jesus lived and behaved, so we've been doing some reflection on the life of Jesus and nonviolence with our community . . . . There are Muslims and Jews who are participating in (this nonviolent) movement.'" [2.] Stewardship is about taking the difficult path of nonviolence, it is about a commitment to relationship, and the self-sacrifice of redemptive love. Stewardship asks the question what will we leave behind for our children.

What should our stewardship look like? How can we turn around Jane Goodall's comment that we as humans have not been very good stewards? First, stewardship is self-sacrifice, not self-destruction. It is self-giving for the well being of one another just as Jesus gave of himself for the life of the world. "Who are these robed in white?" asked an elder in the lesson from Revelation. They have come out of the great ordeal, the struggle of life, by grace and by self-giving love. That is the commitment we want to leave for our children. It is the very opposite of hatred. It is our stewardship.

Stewardship is also the opposite of arrogance, of believing that one does not need the other. "Blessed are the poor in spirit," Jesus said, "for theirs is the kingdom of heaven." And similarly, blessed are the meek, blessed are the merciful or forgiving, blessed are the peacemakers. Jesus is describing a community marked by modesty—each one aware of their need for God. Each one aware that only in community can they meet this need. This too is stewardship.

Stewardship is a time of gathering together. "Do not damage the earth or the sea or the trees," the angel called out in the Book of Revelation. Stewardship is our care for all creation until all—all nations, all tribes, all peoples and languages—are gathered together. Stewardship is staying in relationship even when it is hard and we disagree. At Diocesan Convention this weekend a group of us heard from a Palestinian and a Jew, both Americans, both PhD's, both have been friends for ten years and both disagree completely with one another. The Palestinian addressed his friend's concern for security: "Security comes about from how we treat one another." And, "If Jews and Palestinians do not sit and talk," he said, "then the future is very dark." Stewardship is our commitment to a common destiny. We are "knit together" in the words of our prayer, whether we like it or not. All life on earth is deeply interconnected. We want to leave our children this sense of the common good.

Today we gather in our pledges to God through the mission of the church. And yes it is a pledge of the money we will give for the coming year. But if that is all it is we miss what is most important. What we give to God is an act of love. It is the very opposite of terror. When we give we recognize a higher power in our life and the legitimacy of others. Stewardship brings with it a modesty that is a blessing. When we give for one another's good we express a commitment to relationship. This is our pledge—compassion that is stronger than loss, the blessing of modesty, and the relatedness of all things. It is our orientation to life now, our hope for the future, and our gift to the children.

Amen.

Notes:

1. Dr. Jane Goodall addressed the *Science and the Spiritual Quest Boston Conference* via telecast on Monday, October 22, 2001 on the subject of "What Does It Mean to Be Human?" held at The Memorial Church of Harvard University.

2. The priest is Naim Stifan Ateek, a Palestinian Christian who is the founder and head of the Sabeel Ecumenical Liberation Theology Center in Jerusalem. The quote may have been from *The Witness* magazine. His latest book, *A Palestinian Christian Cry for Reconciliation*, was published by Orbis in 2008.

Ecclesiasticus 44: 1-10, 13-14
Revelation 7: 2-4, 9-17
Matthew 5: 1-12

2006

"Stepping Stones"

5 Epiphany/February 5, 2006

"(Jesus) came and took her by the hand and lifted her up."—Mark 1: 31

In the most recent issue of the parish newsletter, Jim Trimble [1] alluded to the fact that I do not walk on water—and it is true, and a good thing to be reminded of. It does make me think of a story about a priest, a rabbi and a little boy. They all went fishing and were out for a very long time. The priest had to answer nature's call so he excused himself, got out of the boat, and walked across the water to the shore behind some bushes. He returned to his place in the boat the same way. Later, the rabbi, in answer to the same need, excused himself, walked across the water and soon came back. Meanwhile the boy's eyes grew about as big as saucers. He decided he was going to try it too. He stepped out of the boat, fell into the water way over his head and came up sputtering. The priest turned to the rabbi and commented rather matter of factly, he hasn't learned yet where the stepping-stones are.

We need to find those places, the solid rock, that will support us and keep us from getting in over our heads. There are two women and a man in the Bible readings today that show us where the stepping-stones are, where we can walk without getting overwhelmed.

First, there is the Shunamite woman. She is self-assured and assertive, displaying both caution and tenderness. Elisha grants her a child which is more than she could hope for. Years pass and the boy accompanies his father into a field. There he finds himself in severe pain and being carried home, apparently dies on his mother's lap. It is hard to imagine any more overwhelming shock or deeper distress. What catches my attention is how she finds the strength to say, "It will be alright." To her husband she says, "It will be alright." To the prophet's servant she says, "It is alright." She somehow has found the faith described in the Book of Hebrews as "the assurance of things hoped for, the conviction of things not seen." It will be alright, she asserts. And in some remarkable way, it was. She found a stepping-stone, the rock of faith, upon which she could stand.

Lest we think the Shunamite woman unique, another woman, an anchorite of the 14th century named Julian of Norwich had much the same experience. She lived during the Black Plague and the Hundred Years' War. She found herself meditating on sin, which can be as dark and overwhelming as loss. Rather than despair she heard Jesus in a vision say to her, "all shall be well, and all shall be well, and all manner of thing shall be well." [2] It nearly echoes the words of the Shunamite woman, "It will be alright." We all need this faith upon which to stand and be upheld.

The Apostle Paul can tell us of another stepping-stone. He has discovered an empathy that allows him to relate to all people in many different circumstances. He desires to win them not to one side or another but to Christ, that unconditional compassion upon which all can stand. Oh, Paul was trained in taking sides. As a Pharisee he learned that one was either ritually pure or else profane. We, as well, are no strangers to this line of thought. We say, "you are either for us or against us." You are either friend or foe, trustworthy or terrorist. Someone described this way of thinking as a dual polarity paradigm. No fight, no news, is the way some in the media put it. And often this feels so overwhelming. Paul looked beyond this paradigm. He was able to empathize with those on every side, not to leave them where they were but to introduce them to Christ's reign that is the mending of creation, not its division. This empathy to win others for the sake of mending is another of those stepping-stones that holds us up.

Lest we think Paul unique, we were given another example just this week of one whose empathy for the down-trodden caused her to sing and speak out for justice. Coretta Scott King could have retreated to the needs of her own family and to her own grief after her husband's murder and no one would have remarked about it. But she possessed the empathy to look beyond her kinship circle to see others wounded by racism, diminished by poverty, and done in by violence. She, like her husband, desired to win others to a compassion that was not just for one people or another. She would seek God's will which is the well being of *all* people.

Finally, there is Simon Peter's mother-in-law. She opens her hand so that it can be grasped by Jesus, who then may lift her up. Hope is this active openness, this waiting for Jesus' grasp. Paul says in Romans, that we hope for what we do not see and we wait for it with patience. Simon's mother-in-law had this open-handed, receptive hope. And Jesus lifted her up. All too often we live life with a closed fist. We have to get by on our own, to be beholden to no one. This is an aloneness, that when up against it, can be very overwhelming. Hope is another one of those stepping-stones that hold us up.

Paul describes these stepping-stones as the greater gifts. "Faith, hope, and love," he says "abide, these three"—the faith of the Shunamite woman, the hope of Simon's mother-in-law, and the love or empathy of Paul. As in the story of the priest, the rabbi, and the little boy we need to learn where these stepping-stones are, if we are not to get in over our heads.

The Christian life is a practice, like medicine or the law. We are continually growing and refining our abilities. How we do this is to walk more and more readily on these three stones. We cannot stand on the rock of faith without being part of a faith community. It is the community that encourages us to grow and stand upon our faith. At the same time that we practice being in community, we need to look outside our own group or family and empathize with others. We are all meant to be in search of God's kingdom which is a world-wide mending. Finally, we need to practice hope which is that receptive openness to being grasped by God. "Precious Lord," Coretta King sang, "take my hand. Lead me on, let me stand"—on faith, on love, on hope, not overwhelmed but lifted up.

Amen.

Notes:

1. The Rev. James Trimble, former rector of Old Christ Church in Philadelphia, served as Interim priest at Saint Paul's in 2005.

2. Julian of Norwich, *Revelations of Divine Love,* translated by M. L. Del Mastro, Garden City: Image Books, 1977, p. 124 (Chapter 27).

2Kings 4: 8-37
1Corinthians 9: 16-23
Mark 1: 29-39

"I Can See the Cross in You"

Palm Sunday/April 9, 2006

"Let the same mind be in you that was in Christ Jesus."—Philippians 2: 5

"Let the same mind be in you that was in Christ Jesus," Paul said. We are each to reveal the likeness of Christ. A Sunday School teacher was telling me of the Godly Play class on the faces of Christ. Now the great thing about Godly Play is that instead of being *told* who God is, which is how most of us were taught, in Godly Play children *discover* who God is. In the class, the teacher showed pictures of faces, and a picture of Jesus' face. She asked if the children could see the cross in those faces. One little girl, again probably like most of us, had the hardest time. She just couldn't see it. Then after a long pause the girl smiled and said, "I get it." The nose is the vertical piece, and the eyes form the cross bar. In each of the facial pictures she could see the cross. But not only that, she looked up from the pictures and said, "I can see the cross in you." What a wonderful discovery—that our children can begin to find the cross in one another. "Let the same mind be in you that was in Christ Jesus."

The French Artist, Georges Roualt, painted this same experience. After a brilliant career his work, perhaps because of its spiritual quality and its willingness to confront suffering, has of late, grown out of fashion. Having lived through the World Wars and the atomic fears of the early Cold War years, he died in 1958. He said, "As a Christian in such hazardous times, I believe only in Jesus on the cross. I am," he said, "a Christian of olden times." [1.] And indeed the cross was at the center of early Christian belief.

One of Roualt's famous paintings was entitled, "La Sainte Face," or the Sacred Face. Here we see Jesus weeping with those who weep (Romans 12:15). In his eyes we perceive the compassion of God. Above his eyes, dark eyebrows intersect with an elongated nose to form a cross in the face of

Christ. On Jesus' face, his sacred face, Christ bears the sign of compassion, that nothing not even death may overcome. Paul says, "Let the same mind be in you that was in Christ Jesus." And the little girl says, "I can see the cross in you." We are all marked by the cruciform sign of God's compassion.

Roualt concluded that in hazardous times, and what times aren't, suffering is inevitable, yet it need not be isolating. Suffering, instead, may be the passage to hope. The Benedictine Laurence Freeman suggests that passion means "passing through." We understand what the Passion means by asking ourselves "what are we really going through at this moment?" Can we read the cross in our face? If we can, then suffering becomes a bridge connecting us with God and others. We discover God's compassion and become more compassionate. This Passion, the passing through from suffering to compassion, is the priority in the Gospel of Mark.

It is not the priority in our culture. Instead of looking for the cross in others, we see them peer back at us in magazines with unblemished beauty setting for us an impossible standard. Instead of a cruciform face, society puts on an ideal face that no one can really live up to. Young people, for instance, may succumb to eating disorders to attain the desired look. Adults try to have it all only to discover, or perhaps never discover, that they have lost something in the process. Others missing the advertised riches and beauty feel the less for it. Our culture has disfigured some persons beyond the possibility of their esteeming their own self-worth correctly.

The lesson of the Palm Sunday Passion is to see in ourselves and in others the Sacred Face. Like the little girl in Godly Play we may look up and exclaim, "I can see the cross in you." The lesson of the Palm Sunday Passion is to see others passing through to greater and greater compassion. And by God's grace others may see the same in us. It is not an impossible standard, but starts with what we are really going through. Jesus accompanies us. Our faces are both cruciform. Our destinies are both compassion. We can reckon our self-worth correctly in that we are both God's beloved. "I can see the cross in you," each says to the other. "Let the same mind be in (us) that was in Christ Jesus."

Amen.

Notes:

1. Booty, John, *The Christ We Know*, Cambridge: Cowley Publications, 1987, p. 91ff.

Isaiah 52: 13-53: 12
Philippians 2: 5-11
Mark 15: 1-39

"Larry King Live and a Father's Love"

The Second Sunday after Pentecost/June 18, 2006

> *"(Jesus) also said, 'With what can we compare the kingdom of God, or what parable will we use for it? It is like a mustard seed, which, when sown upon the ground, is the smallest of all the seeds on earth . . . '"—Mark 4: 30-31*

"With what can we compare the kingdom of God?" Jesus asked. When Jesus prayed, "Our Father . . . thy kingdom come," what did he mean? I imagine that for Jesus to address God as Father can only mean that his own father about whom we know so little must have been a most endearing person. About another father someone said, "When Dad entered the room, the whole world made sense." Joseph must have made that kind of impact on his son, Jesus. In fact, the word that Jesus most often used for God, who was like a father to him, was the Aramaic word *Abba*. This word does not translate into English but the closest we can come is the familiar name, "Dad."

Can we look at Joseph and today's parables and get an idea of how Jesus understood God? We first meet Joseph when he is betrothed to Mary. Mary is expecting a child who is not Joseph's own. Nevertheless, Joseph makes room for this boy naming him Jesus. By exercising his right to name the child, Joseph acknowledges his wife's son as his own and he becomes Jesus' legal father.

Eight days after Jesus' birth as was the custom, Joseph and Mary presented and named their child in the Temple. A man by the name of Simeon, guided by the Holy Spirit, met them and gathered up Jesus in his arms. He sings a song of praise. Joseph and Mary were amazed at what was said about their son. Their love will have to be one of letting be if this child is to become a light and glory for the Gentiles and Israel. Then sometime before Jesus reached the age of thirty his father, his *abba,* died. But not before teaching Jesus the true meaning of a father's love.

Jesus teaches by parables that God's love, like his father's, has to do with "making room" and "letting be." First, making room. The kingdom of God is like a mustard seed that becomes the greatest of all shrubs. Jesus is being funny. He is using humor to say something true. The great world tree in which all may take shelter is usually likened to the tall, majestic cedars. No one expects the mustard bush to be compared with the cedars of Lebanon. It is ludicrous. I am reminded of Peter Sellers' movie *The Mouse that Roared* where the tiny, impoverished nation of Grand Fenwick invades Central Park in the greatest city of the world's greatest country. So Jesus' kingdom of love (tiny as a mustard seed) has invaded the giant Empire of Rome. But this is not so impossible as it seems. The Prophet Ezekiel warns that the high and lofty cedar (in his day it was Egypt, like Assyria before) will fall and great will be its fall. Jesus' tiny seed, however, will grow to such a great bush that the "birds of the air can make nests in its shade." The love of God is elastic, it stretches, it makes room so that all can belong, all can find a place. "In my Father's house there are many dwelling places," Jesus taught. As Jesus' father made room for him, so Jesus' God makes room for all.

A second parable teaches about "letting be." The parable Jesus chooses to tell is about the seed that grows. The scattered seed has an innate and independent purposefulness. The sower cannot control what plant it will become. That is inherent in the created seed. Nor can the sower be in control of the outcome. The phrasing, "sleep and rise, night and day, sprout and grow" conveys an independent rhythm apart from the life of the sower. For his or her part, the sower must let be and trust in the power and goodness of God who has ordered creation for the well-being of all.

Theologically we can say God is Holy Being, not a being among others but the source of all being and as personal as Jesus' *abba*. Nothing could exist without God's letting it be. God's love is self-giving. That is, God gives God's very being. Holy Being gives everything else its existence. Growth involves a drive toward authenticity. Love gives the space in which one may grow more and more into the likeness of Christ. Evil, on the other hand, is what interferes with this letting be and consequent growth. One might think of suffocating expectations or coercive manipulation that push us out of shape, distort life and keep it from being authentic.

So when we talk about God the Father we are not so much making a gender distinction as saying that the meaning of God's love is "making room" and "letting be." As parents we know how hard that is. We marvel at Joseph and Mary. As a church we are struggling with how to express that love. At a coffee shop the other day on the Avenue someone turned to me and asked if I was Anglican. I said I was and then he asked if I had seen the Larry King Show the night before. I had to confess sheepishly that I was asleep by then. Back at the office I downloaded the transcript and saw that there had been an interesting conversation among Bishop Gene Robinson of New Hampshire, Canon David Anderson of the Anglican American Council, a Roman Catholic priest and Baptist seminary president, a columnist and a congregational minister, with Presiding Bishop Frank Griswold present for part of the show. The topic of course was the place of Gay and Lesbian Christians in the church.

I could not help but place that conversation in the context of what Jesus is trying to tell us about God, his *abba,* whose love is one of making room, as Joseph made room for Jesus, as the comparatively small mustard shrub makes room for all creatures, as the Father's house has many dwelling places. The Father's love also lets us be so that we can grow true, more and more who we are in the likeness of Christ. On this day I could not help but think of another father who gave words to this love in what is one of the shortest and most memorable inaugural addresses in American history. Perhaps it is no accident that our General Convention is still struggling with the aftermath of the war over which he presided. His words are words of love that make room and let be. He said, "With malice toward none; with charity for all; with firmness in the right, as God gives us to see the right, let us strive on to finish the work (of) . . . a lasting peace, among ourselves, and with all nations."

Amen.

Notes:

1. Lincoln, Abraham, "Second Inaugural Address" (March 4, 1865), in *Words that Made American History: Colonial Times to the 1870s,* edited by Richard N. Current and John A. Garraty, Boston: Little Brown and Company, 1965, p. 538.

Ezekiel 31: 1-6, 10-14
2Corinthians 5: 1-10
Mark 4: 26-34

"Violence or Mending: the Forbidden Fruit or the Bread of Life?"

The Tenth Sunday after Pentecost/August 13, 2006

"Therefore keep the commandments of the Lord your God, by walking in his ways and by fearing him."—Deuteronomy 8: 6

We keep God's commandments, the Book of Deuteronomy says, by "walking in God's ways." Forgiveness is the glue that holds us together. We forgive one another, as Paul says, the way God in Christ has forgiven us. In the confession of sin that we will say in a few moments, the whole point of repentance is to "delight in God's will, and walk in God's ways, to the glory of God's Name." There is nothing sorrowful or severe in our community. Rather it is about delight and glory and following God's ways that lead to the renewal of creation—a mended, beautiful and just world. This is not just a blind hope. We are given the assurance of Jesus' resurrection. He indeed is living bread, the promise of life forever.

In contrast to this, and weighing heavily on my heart this summer, has been the violence in our city and our world. I refuse to accept violence as a fact of life. As Christians we decry it and seek nourishment from the bread of life. This week in a program at Drexel University 37 teenagers are studying the violence in their neighborhoods. Killings have taken over 230 lives in Philadelphia in the first half of this year. Our city is on track to exceed last year's 377 murders mostly of young people between the ages of 18 and 24. The youth studying at Drexel realize that we cannot accept violence as a way of life; we need to curtail it and be nourished instead by the bread of life. On Thursday, British police stopped an al-Qaeda-like plan to use liquid explosives to destroy ten planes in the air. Not even religion is exempt from the enticement of violence. As religious people we can make no peace with violence, but must instead walk in God's ways made known to us in the Prince of Peace, the Bread of Life. Violence has even seeped down to the level of our conversation. In one place, I know of an insecure person whose opening gambit is typically one of anger. Then only after he has backed everyone off can something of a conversation begin. Paul wants to know what we will do with our anger? Will we allow it to fester? Will we use it to belittle and distance others? If we do, Paul says, we are "grieving" the Holy Spirit. Any violence done to community and fellowship is a sorrow to God. We confess our violence, refusing to make it a way of life. God's way is our walk, God's will is our delight, and God's Name is our glory.

The contrast between the world's violence and the world's renewal can be made no clearer than by the forbidden fruit of Genesis and the Bread of Life in John. In the Genesis story Adam and Eve in the Garden of Eden have everything at their disposal (they lack for nothing) except they must not eat of the tree of the knowledge of good and evil. The point of the prohibition is they are not to seek wisdom without submission to their Creator. Violence is often a way of trying to take control of our lives on our own, without relying on God. In contrast, Jesus says: the renewed creation, a non-violent world, has already begun in me. "I am the bread of life." Whoever eats this bread, whoever partakes of me, whoever submits to God, becomes part of the world's mending and others' well being.

The entire sweep of the Bible portrays the way in which God's people are to walk, from self-serving control and coercion (often violent) to healing and life (always nourishing). We who have joined ourselves to Jesus have work to do. Jesus' description of himself as the bread of life denotes the first grain of a final harvest still to come—an ingathering of justice and peace. We have our part to play, partnering with God, to bring in this new day. "What can we do?" What can 37 teenagers do to stop violence in Philadelphia? What can anyone of us do to change the climate of terror that makes security so critical? How is it possible for anger to be creative rather than destructive? How can we stop grieving the Holy Spirit? How can we begin to partake of and share the bread of life?

The answer Paul gives is to live in love, just as Jesus gave of himself in love for the life of the world. We are to imitate God in love, and in God's forgiveness when we fall short. Whatever we do, whether of great import or minor, when compared to God, will be small. Do not be dispirited. Have courage and persistence. What matters most is that we not accept violence as a fact of life. The renewal of creation has already begun. The good that we do today in the name of Christ and in the power of the Spirit—no matter how small it seems to us—will not be lost on the world. God is able to use it for the creation's mending.

So what does God want us to do? There is a helpful story from the Native American tradition. A Cherokee elder was teaching her grandchildren about life. She said to them, "A fight is going on inside me . . . it is a terrible fight, and it is between two wolves. One wolf represents violence, killing, terror, unrestrained anger, control and coercion, fear and hatred. The other wolf stands for community, forgiveness, delight, hope, life, renewal and mending, justice and peace. She added, this same fight is going on inside you, and inside every other person, too." They thought about it for a minute and then one child asked his grandmother, "Which wolf will win?" The old Cherokee woman simply replied . . . "The one that you feed."

God wants us to feed community and a mending world by partaking of the bread of life. We are identified not by whom we hate but by whom we love. In submitting ourselves to Christ all are one. We feed community by being members of one another over many years. We can teach a child not to hit, but it takes a lot of time and experience in community to achieve a mature understanding of peace. We feed community by modeling a commitment to life and love. No one person will model everything that is true, but because we are a community, many people will manifest one facet or another facet that when all pieced together give a glimpse of the recreated world of God. Let's not make do with violence but feed the world with the bread of life.

Amen.

Notes:

Deuteronomy 8: 1-10
Ephesians 4: 30-5: 2
John 6: 37-51

2007

"The Workplace is Holy"

The Fifth Sunday after the Epiphany/February 4, 2007

> *"Now the angel of the Lord came and sat under the oak at Ophrah, which belonged to Joash the Abiezrite, as his son Gideon was beating out wheat in the wine press, to hide it from the Midionites."*—Judges 6: 11

What strikes me about the scriptures this morning is how holy is our workplace. It seems an odd pairing: sacredness and work. There is an apocryphal story told of John F. Kennedy campaigning in West Virginia. A miner interrupted him with a question. "Is it true that you haven't done an honest day's hard labor in your life?" The would-be president abashedly admitted as much and waited for the second shoe to drop. The miner just stepped up and shook his hand and said, "Believe me, you haven't missed a thing." This represents the usual way we think of work. We would hardly call it holy!

But here we find Gideon beating out wheat, separating the chaff, keeping his work secret from the competition. In this case, he fears a hostile take-over by Midianites whose innovation was the use of camels to sweep in from the desert upon unsuspecting villagers. God meets Gideon in his covert workplace and declares: "I will be with you," and my peace as well. To emphasize the holiness of this threshing place, Gideon builds an altar there and calls it "The Lord is peace."

Jesus goes into a workplace as well to reveal God's extravagant grace and to call three of his disciples. He gets into Simon's fishing boat. This is not a recreational craft, but all business—fish scales and folded nets, no amenities. It is a workboat. It is here Jesus teaches, demonstrates God's grace and calls. It is often said that the ceiling of the nave of a church is like the up-side-down hull of a ship. The word nave, or central part of a church, comes from the Medieval Latin *navis* that means ship. The nave of a church is also no recreational craft, but it's a workboat where Jesus teaches, demonstrates and calls. In each instance, the workplace is holy, and the sacred is a place of work.

In the letter to the Colossians we read, "Whatever your task, put yourselves into it, as done for the Lord and not for your masters . . . <u>you</u> serve the Lord Christ" (Col. 3: 23-24). Martin Luther King took as an example what is usually considered a menial job to make this point. "If a man is called to be a street sweeper, he should sweep streets even as Michelangelo painted, or Beethoven composed music, or Shakespeare wrote poetry. He should sweep streets so well that all the hosts of heaven and earth will pause to say, here lived a great street sweeper who did his job well." Work is holy whether threshing, fishing, sweeping, lawyering, teaching, selling, financing, care-giving, in whatever ways we work. Just as Jesus climbed into a workboat, so he enters every work place to teach, demonstrate grace and call.

This does not mean that we should be reading the Bible when we should be reading financial forecasts, or handing out tracts when we should be handing out a prospectus. But the Bible and spiritual understanding do effect for the better how we carry out our jobs. Work is holy. The second creation story has the Lord God placing the human creature in the Garden of Eden to till it (Gen. 2: 15). This is before any disobedience. There is something holy about our work.

Here are some workplace insights from the lessons today.

- First, God takes what is small and calls it mighty. Gideon is the least of the weakest clan and God calls him a mighty warrior. Paul is the least of the apostles but the grace of God is with him. In the same way we need not shrink from tasks that are demanding, meager and hesitant as we might be.
- Jesus is playful. He is in a fishing boat and wants to see what it can do. Let's take it out into the deep and let down the nets. Experiment, try things, play, see what can happen.
- The corollary to this willingness to experiment is an openness to unseen grace. No one in Simon's fishing boat can perceive what is under the surface. Who knows what will come up? Expect the unexpected. Grace is not guaranteed success, but God's free acceptance and esteem of each one of us through faith.

- This grace is superabundant. God's forgiveness is overflowing. We are lifted up in rebirth and renewal. We are always hopeful. There is a phrase, that God makes a way out of no way. There is no way that Gideon should defeat the Midianites. There is no way that Paul should be called an apostle. There is no way that Simon should find any fish. But each one sets out because of God's extravagant promise to be with them.
- The best leadership has a quality of humility. Arrogance is off putting. With humility Peter will begin to catch people, to draw them to the good news of grace. Peter falling down at Jesus' knees is a gesture of humility. It is in humility that Paul can say, "by the grace of God I am what I am" nothing more, nothing less. The best leaders have this quality of humility.
- Finally, when work is holy it is purposeful. Jesus knows what a fishing boat is for. Peter's new purpose will be to catch people, to draw them up to new life in Christ. Our work, whatever it is, has purpose in God's plan of service, renewal, well-being and community. Purpose is what makes us proud.

How holy is our workplace! This week the scriptures call us to look for Jesus in our places of work. Whether it is a paying job or not, we are all tilling some ground. Jesus enters our job site to teach, demonstrate God's grace and call. Lift one another up. Draw one another to a life-giving purpose. Be playful, and uncover a grace so extravagant that it will seem heaven and earth have paused to say here lives workers of faith who are doing their jobs well.

Amen.

Notes:

Judges 6: 11-24a
1Corinthians 15: 1-11
Luke 5: 1-11

"Racism and Uprootedness"

The Sixth Sunday after the Epiphany/February 11, 2007

"They shall be like a shrub in the desert, / and shall not see when relief comes. / They shall live in the parched places of the wilderness, / in an uninhabited salt land."—Jeremiah 17: 6

King Tut and the Golden Age of the Pharaohs came to Philadelphia last week. The history of ancient Egypt and Israel intertwines at a number of points. King Tut would have ruled Egypt in 1333 before the Common Era as part of the 18th dynasty about 40 years after the Exodus when tradition has the Israelites escaping from slavery there. A century later in the 19th dynasty, around 1200, we have a document called "the Wisdom or Instruction of Amen-em-opet." This bears some striking similarity to the prophecy of Jeremiah given some 600 years later. As King Tut comes to Philadelphia we are reminded of an ancient wisdom that is particularly poignant today.

Jeremiah dismisses those who put their trust in mere mortals and make mere flesh their strength. If we are rooted in ourselves we become actually rootless like a shrub in the desert. I imagine something like tumbleweed. Instead of fleshly trust in the transitory, the Wisdom of Amen-em-opet denounces the hotheaded person, perhaps misplaced trust and hotheadedness are not so dissimilar. The one is like a desert shrub, the other is like a tree grown indoors says Amen-em-opet. Neither one is particularly well rooted.

Given this context, the recent comment by the U.S. Senator from Delaware, Joe Biden, is understandable. As everyone knows by now, Biden said of Barak Obama as a presidential candidate, he is "the first mainstream African-American who is articulate and bright . . ." What African-Americans heard was that it is surprising that someone of color is articulate. Biden has a way of inadvertently shining a spotlight on my unexamined assumptions of being white. A scholar from Wellesley, Peggy McIntosh who is also white says in the United States whiteness is like having an invisible knapsack provisioned with presumptions that one is articulate, possesses leadership, has access to places one wishes to go, and options that one may choose from without considering whether one's own race would be accepted. [1.] These privileges are hidden until someone like Joe Biden misspeaks. As a white person in this culture I am a little like Amen-em-opet's tree grown indoors. There are cultural blinders that are like walls. Shouldn't everyone be like me? It feels normal to have a privileged position in the corner of the room. Then when we meet someone from outside, we may express surprise at their qualities that are equal to or greater than our own, or we are free not to pay attention. When we comment upon the abilities of people of color, that they should have them, it is faint praise indeed. Carrying this invisible knapsack of privilege is, as Jeremiah said, making mere flesh, that is the color of our skin, our strength. Jesus taught, woe be to those whose invisible knapsack is filled with unearned power and unfair advantage yielding riches, fullness, laughter and acclaim.

Some years ago I was talking with Cecily O'Bryant whose late husband John had been the first African American to be elected to the Boston School Committee. We were talking about the prejudices we had growing up. Everyone has prejudices, negative attitudes based on prejudgment from one's own or one's group's point of view. Racism is different in that it carries an unearned and systemic power to hold down another because of race. So Cecily and I were talking, treading on sensitive ground. I said when I was a boy I believed and thought it commonly assumed by those around me that in football, blacks could not play quarterback. Cecily looked at me astonished. Her eyes began to twinkle. Her lips began to twitch. Finally, she couldn't control herself and burst out laughing and said, "Cliff, that is the most foolish thing I have ever heard." And it was. I had been an "indoor tree," sheltered by race in a way that allowed me at the time not to question a silly and oppressive assumption.

Now what makes this different from prejudice is the power involved that kept many fine athletes from playing this leadership and skill position until the assumption became untenable and there were Warren Moon, Randall Cunningham, and now Donovan McNabb, Michael Vick, Vince Young and on and on. I had had no training in seeing myself as an unfairly advantaged person. I wonder what other assumptions about race are equally untenable?

Racism diminishes the society or community that holds it. If one is free to ignore a portion of the whole, everyone is diminished. If one is set up in a privileged corner of a room, or grounded in oneself one becomes groundless, insufficiently rooted. It distorts one's humanity.

What Jesus wants us to do is to shine a spotlight on the invisible knapsack of privilege so that it is no longer invisible and can be unpacked. Instead of unearned advantage, it needs to be filled with unearned grace, that divine acceptance and esteem that is freely showered on everyone. Jesus wants us to take down the walls so that there are no more poorly rooted, artificially sheltered indoor trees, to use Amen-em-opet's metaphor. Articulateness then is not a presumption of skin color but earned through education of many different forms by many different people. Watch how Jesus unpacks the knapsack of privilege.

Blessed are you who are poor (with an empty "knapsack"). Why? Because God will mend you, and God will use us to be agents of one another's mending. Blessed are you who hunger, and recognize the hunger of others. God will fill you with the passion to care for those in need. Blessed are those who weep. This is the conversion of tears. We see suffering and exclaim, "Dear God." We find in God's power of renewal and healing the energy to laugh. Finally, blessed are you when you are excluded. Why? Because we then discover compassion for those on the outside. We cease to be indoor trees of privilege and begin to take down the walls of separation.

The coming of King Tut to Philadelphia puts us in touch with an ancient wisdom as old as the Bible itself, echoed by Jeremiah, expanded upon by Jesus and as true today as ever. Joe Biden's comment on the articulateness of someone of color, my memory of athletes of color excluded from leadership, the way race has impacted each of us and continues to do so, needs to be unpacked. In the space that is left there is an emptiness for God to fill. That is why Jesus declares, bereft of unearned privilege, we are surprisingly blessed. In the metaphor of Jeremiah and Amen-em-opet, our roots, no longer pinched, will be able to expand and sink down and intermingle in the communion of One who gave himself for all that each may have life and that in abundance.

Amen.

Notes:

1. McIntosh, Peggy, "White Privilege and Male Privilege: A Personal Account of Coming to See Correspondences through Work in Women's Studies," *Working Papers Series,* No. 189, Wellesley: Center for Research on Women, 1988.

Jeremiah 17: 5-10
1Corinthians 15: 12-20
Luke 6: 17-26

"Mother Teresa and God's Absence"

The Fourteenth Sunday after Pentecost/September 2, 2007

"For all who exalt themselves will be humbled, and those who humble themselves will be exalted."—Luke 14: 11

"When you give a banquet," Jesus said, "invite the poor." No one lived out that charge more fully than Mother Teresa. Her life both raises questions and gives an example for our faith. "When you give a banquet, invite the poor." In Jesus' time, table fellowship, as in gathering for a banquet, expressed an intimate relation among those assembled. Obviously Jesus wants our intimacy and care to extend expressly to the poor. The moment of intimacy for Mother Teresa with Jesus happened at the age of 36 on a train ride to Darjeeling in the Himalayan foothills. Christ spoke to her and said, "Come be my light." Set up a banquet of compassion in the slums of the city. Never again would Teresa be granted such closeness with Jesus. And ever after would she be longing for it.

Come Be My Light, is also the title of a collection of Mother Teresa's letters that is due out on Tuesday. Some of the letters are dark, full of Christ's absence and Teresa's desperate longing. Ten years after her close, personal experience of Jesus she wrote of Christ's absence, "Such deep longing for God—and . . . repulsed—empty—no faith—no love—no zeal." The irony is that when Mother Teresa hosted her banquet for the poor, Jesus was powerfully present to them and to the world, and just as powerfully absent from her. When Mother Teresa answered Jesus' call to be his light in the slums of the city, Christ's light shown for the poor and the world, and was dark to her.

How do we understand God's absence? Is it, as some atheists claim, all a human fabrication anyway? Or is something deeper going on? The *Song of Solomon* in the Old Testament is a love poem between a young woman and a man. It is often explored mystically as our relation with God. The young couple's love is sensual and full. Then the woman dreams of her Beloved, "I opened to my beloved, but my beloved had turned and was gone . . . . I sought him, but did not find him; I called him, but he gave no answer" (Song 5: 6). There is something in the Beloved's absence that evokes yearning, following, journeying after, the ache for the one who is missing and the willingness to pursue.

A Welsh poet who died just a few years ago was known for his exploration of God's absence. In one of R. S. Thomas' poems entitled "Sea-Watching"[1] he evokes the image of a bird watcher wearing out his eyes as Mother Teresa must have worn out her knees, watching, waiting, looking, praying for this rare bird, the Holy Spirit. "Ah," Thomas explains, "but a rare bird is/ rare. It is when one is not looking,/ at times one is not there/ that it comes." God's absence, Thomas concludes, presumes a presence, the presence of One who has just left or is about to come. The long fast of the rare bird's absence has focused the watcher's mind on this singular endeavor. The bird's absence, he said, was its presence.

Lover, bird watcher, we all understand something about absence. Nevertheless, we are left with a question. How can we be sure of our faith when we see God in someone like Teresa for whom God is absent? How she struggles! Shouldn't faith make life easier and not harder? In our culture of convenience, it is difficult to understand faith. If faith is a pursuit, a race to be run as Paul often said, if it constitutes hospitality toward those in prison, "as though you were in prison with them" as Hebrews teaches, then faith does not make life easier. How then can we be so sure of our faith, how can we trust it enough to exert ourselves and give ourselves to it?

First, we can entrust ourselves to faith because of God's promise. We hear this promise in the Letter to the Hebrews, God says: "I will never leave you or forsake you." Even when God is absent, we have the promise, "I will never leave you." Even when we begin a venture where the outcome is so uncertain as entering slums with nothing, to minister to the poor who have nothing—"I will never forsake you." Even in Christ's God-forsakenness on the cross, God did not leave him. Rather, God raised him just as Jesus taught: "Friend, move up higher." This is the second reason to give ourselves to faith: God's work in Jesus. The resurrection is life out of death, forgiveness out of wrong. We not only have the promise, we have what God has already done in Jesus and that is God's free gift of life to us today. Finally, we can give ourselves to faith because of the others who have done so. We have seen in their action the good, the dignity, the life and compassion that results. Mother Teresa's life for all its struggle influenced many. One was a Ugandan, Timothy Wangusa, who wrote a poem entitled, "Mother Teresa's Wish." [2] He imagines her response to the Nobel Peace Prize banquet in Oslo in 1979. She apologizes for her absence then asks everyone to send the banquet's equivalent "in cash/ To provide 400 of the city's poorest poor/ With lunch and supper for 366 days." "When you give a banquet," Jesus said, "invite the poor."

I heard Mother Teresa speak in 1976 twenty years after she wrote of being repulsed, empty, no zeal. Her struggle with Christ's absence had been going on a long time. She was in Philadelphia for the Eucharistic Congress that year, and told of seeing a lone, teen-aged Philadelphia boy sitting on a stone wall. He was for her an icon of what she called the West's spiritual poverty—separation, disconnection, work places without loyalty to workers, families without time for one another, a boy sitting on a wall. Teresa's mind was singularly focused on overcoming impoverishment, economic and spiritual. Perhaps she could identify with the poor because of the absence that ached within. She lived out that ache as a pursuit of her Beloved.

Our faith too is a pursuit with all its ups and downs. Hopefully for most of us, not quite as intense as for Teresa. We can and do give ourselves to such a faith pursuit because of God's **work** of resurrection, God's **promise** to be present even in absence, and because of the **action** of others. We never banquet at the Lord's table here without being aware of the poor we serve in our own city, of the homeless we care for within our own walls, of the presence of our own youth with young people of the Sioux tribe on the Standing Rock Reservation, of the presence of those who are alone and without community in our own society. "Whenever you give a banquet," Jesus said, "invite the poor."

Amen.

Notes:

1. Thomas, R. S., *Poems of R. S. Thomas*, Fayetteville: The University of Arkansas Press, 1985; p. 107.

2. Wangusa, Timothy, *a pattern of dust: Selected Poems 1965-1990*, Kampala: Fountain Publishers Ltd., 1994; p. 49.

Ecclesiasticus 10: 7-18
Hebrews 13: 1-8
Luke 14: 1, 7-14

"God's Dream and the Universal Lie"

The Twelfth Sunday after Pentecost/August 19, 2007

"I have heard what the prophets have said who prophecy lies in my name, saying, 'I have dreamed, I have dreamed!'"—Jeremiah 23: 25

"I have dreamed, I have dreamed," the lying prophets say in Jeremiah. What they have done is put forth *their* dreams as God's word, rather than God's word as their dream! Their dreams were those of having power over others, of replacing God's name with their own, of dominating self-importance, of raising themselves up by putting others down. They imagined they could contain the fire of God's word and wield the Godly hammer that breaks the rocks. But how wrong they were.

The universal lie of dominating self-importance hasn't gone away. A contemporary disk jockey named DJ AM grew up in Philadelphia. He plays at all the fanciest clubs in L.A. and dates well-known celebrities. He has been through alcohol and drug addiction and this past April celebrated his ninth year of sobriety. From his perch above the dance floor at the club's turntable he sees the dreams of lying prophets. The clubs today, he observes, "are a tangible representation of what I like to call the universal lie. It's a place where people pull up in their Porsche, show off their new Marc Jacobs bag or jewelry or, 'Hey, look at me in V.I.P. with five bottles on my table.' All this stuff means I'm someone in God's eyes" they think. "But that's the lie." It is the rock of dominating self-importance that God's word breaks. It is the tissue thin show of success that is consumed in God's fire.

Another dream is being at the top of a hierarchy. This was a matter of course in the Greco-Roman world of Jesus' day. The Emperor claimed to be divine, replacing God's name with his. Under the emperor there was this elaborate system of patronage that passed power on down the line until the peasant class was reached. Under Roman occupation Galilean peasants were triply taxed. They paid tribute to the Roman emperor, taxes to the local Jewish client-king, and a tithe that wasn't always enforceable to the priests in Jerusalem who controlled access to God in the temple. This hierarchical dream still lives. If I am head of my family with all the control that implies, if I am head of my company, if I have risen to the top in the hierarchy of the church, then as DJ AM explains: it must mean "I'm someone in God's eyes. But that's the lie."

Jesus challenges it. And this is where this difficult Gospel passage comes in. We can get a glimpse of Roman family values from the letter to the Colossians. This was written later than Paul by an admirer and tries to show that Christianity is not socially subversive to the culture around it. Hierarchy looms large. This is where we find the instruction, "Wives be subject to your husbands; children obey your parents; slaves obey your earthly masters" (Col. 3: 18ff.). There is nothing here in these rules for Christian households that would be found jarring to the Roman family ethic.

But these are rules that Jesus, and Paul too, challenge. There was much more equality and freedom in the Jewish tradition from which both Paul and Jesus came than in that of Rome. Jesus' message of the kingdom, that great mending of creation, carried this divine dream of equality even further. We are hearing the disruption of hierarchies when Jesus declares, "Do you think that I have come to bring peace to the earth? No, I tell you, but rather division!" It is the breakdown of hierarchy, for the establishment of equality and mutuality. The hierarchy of father over son is disrupted. Mother over daughter is broken down. The pattern of in-laws over in-laws is divided. In Christ hierarchy gives way to equality so that as Paul would say, "There is no longer Jew or Greek, there is no longer slave or free, there is no longer male and female; for all of you are one in Christ Jesus (Gal. 3: 28). We are to interpret the present time, then and now, in terms of equality in Christ.

The creative disruption of hierarchies is happening in the present time in business. I suppose one ought not be surprised that God's dream of equality would play out in every sphere of creation, the corporate world included. A recent book entitled *Wikinomics*[1.] looks back at the ancient slave empires of Greece, Rome, China and the Americas, later feudal kingdoms and current corporations that organize people "into layers of superiors and subordinates." Disrupting this hierarchy is a horizontal movement called "peering." Through the internet, mining companies, household goods manufacturers like Proctor & Gamble, communication and education organizations are welcoming outsiders as peers in contributing knowledge to the production of superior goods. Equality is a way of business and of life that is creative.

So, Jesus says, read the signs of the times. We can interpret the weather, why do we deceive ourselves? We can tell when it is going to rain. Why can't we tell that status objects don't make the person? We can forecast scorching heat from a south wind, why can't we see that hierarchy, command and control, in family and business is counter-productive? Probably because the dreams of lying prophets are still seductive. We are seduced by dreams of power, of winning the lottery, of hierarchical control, of dominating self-importance. We pretend that this is God's word. But as DJ AM has learned, it is the universal lie. Jesus disrupts it. He makes no peace with it. God is not partial to Jew or Greek or other racial categories. God's will is for the well being of all. Family is about mutuality and respect, not about enforcing compliance. Our dreams are not God's word. Rather God's word is our dream. We hear this dream at the beginning of John's Gospel. "In the beginning was the Word, and the Word was with God . . . . What has come into being in him was life, and the life was the light of all people." Not the bling of a Marc Jacobs bag but the far brighter light of God's grace that gives life. Not being at the top of the heap but the open peering or collaboration with others that is creative. It is not just good religion. It is not just good family relations. It is also good business. It is the kingdom of God.

Amen.

Notes:

DJ AM died in late August, 2009 of a drug overdose of the painkiller OxyContin, a relapse in the management of his own recovery. He had had 11 years of sobriety. After critical injuries when a Lear jet in which he was travelling crashed in 2008, he developed problems with pain medications. A reality show for MTV entitled "Gone Too Far" featuring DJ AM intervening in the drug-using world may have further exposed him to the lure and devastation of drugs.

1. Tapscott, Don and Williams, Anthony D., *Wikinomics: How Mass Collaboration Changes Everything;* New York: Portfolio, 2006.

Jeremiah 23: 23-29
Hebrews 12: 1-14
Luke 12: 49-56

Quintet on Community at Saint Paul's

"Identity, or the Soul of Saint Paul's" [1.]

The Conversion of Saint Paul, the Apostle/January 27, 2008

"But get up and stand on your feet; for I have appeared to you for this purpose, to appoint you to serve and testify . . . "—Acts 26: 16

On this Saint Paul's Day, I want to set before us the significance of Paul for our community. When we enter Saint Paul's, we cross a threshold. The threshold is where the bustle of the Avenue, the demands of the household, the anxiety of the economy, and relationships marked by cynicism intermingle with the possibility of transcendence, an opening to shared compassion, in broken bread and common cup, the body and blood of Christ. The threshold in some Celtic traditions is called a thin place, where spiritual and material worlds intermingle; or I've heard it called a high valley where the heights and the lowlands intersect. However we describe it, we step across this kind of threshold when we enter Saint Paul's.

The Apostle Paul found himself at one of those thresholds on the way to Damascus. His low spirit of persecution came up against the heights of compassion. Fellow Jews, followers of Jesus, claimed that Gentiles, without adhering to Jewish purity rules, could be full and equal members of God's people. Faith shaken, Saul reacted violently and became an agent of persecution. He was on his way to Damascus to carry out his plan to rid Judaism of this dangerous new belief. On the way, Saul's world of violent extremism hit Jesus' world of extreme compassion. It was a threshold where Saul met the risen Jesus in person possessing a transformed yet still physical body—wounded and resurrected. Saul was given living proof that Israel's God had vindicated Jesus' openness to all. This so disoriented Saul that he went away to Arabia to sort things out.

When Saul returned to Damascus, he was in a new place with a new name, so complete was his transformation. Now called Paul, his encounter with the risen Jesus contained the message of his new understanding—the resurrected Jesus was the Messiah before whom "every knee should bend" as sung in the hymn Paul liked to quote. In place of purity laws there was now a person's justification by God's grace through faith. Paul had done an about face, a 180^0 turn. I suppose if we are to talk of a conversion, it is this about face that we mean. Paul remained a Jew under the Law all his life. He just believed that God's messianic community had been opened to others not under the Law through faith. It was not a conversion from Jew to Christian. In fact, in his last letter to the Romans, Paul warns Gentile Christians against arrogance toward Jews. Paul knew where that would lead. He had gone down that road of persecution. Perhaps he had the foresight of centuries of anti-Semitism. Rather, Paul reasoned, all are to be humble before the mystery of God's oneness and compassion. Paul's witness was now God's mission of the mending of creation. When we kick against God's goad toward creation's mending, it hurts. And indeed we witness that hurt every day. There is another way, Paul says. He has learned it the hard way—it is the way of Jesus, the way of life.

We cross a threshold when we enter this church. There are stone carvings over our front doors that describe what this threshold is like. On the left is depicted the encounter of Saul with the risen Christ. It tells us that when we walk through these doors we are going to become changed. I fantasize that it is like a warning label. Warning, you are going to meet Jesus here. It is going to change your life, maybe even 180^0. It will work a change in you toward mending, humility, compassion, life in the face of God's mystery and grace. On the right side of this stone tympanum is carved Paul proclaiming God's grace made perfect in our weakness. He is imprisoned in Rome. Perhaps this is a warning too. Because we have faith does not mean that life is going to come easily for us. Faith instead believes that God's grace is sufficient whatever may befall. Paul until the day he dies gives this witness to God's power perfected in weakness (2Cor. 12: 9). It is our witness too when we cross over this threshold back into the world.

There is a particular quality to our witness that comes from this singular community of which we are a part. Saint Paul's Church for over a century and a half has been a place of turning. You can call this conversion or conversation. In any case it is a "turning—each to the other—in Christ." I like to call it our parish vision. This turning is part of the original energy of Saint Paul's. Almost six months to the day after Abraham Lincoln's assassination in Ford's Theatre, southern and northern clergy, enemies only a year earlier, stood before God at the altar of Saint Paul's. They had gathered in Philadelphia for the Episcopal Church's General Convention that year. At my celebration of new ministry in this church almost two years ago, the preacher, President of the Standing Committee, had that week requested the resignation of the Bishop who was our celebrant at the Eucharist. They both were together before God at the altar of Saint Paul's. It is our particular witness as a parish that people of great difference can stand as one before God. In 1865 with so many southern clergy in the church, the rector at that time recalled years later that it seemed a great "omen of peace for the parish." Peace is the second strand of witness that is particular to Saint Paul's. Nearly a hundred years later the parish planted a Northern Red Oak, symbol of faith's strength, in memory of Dag Hammarskjöld and all those who have given their lives for world peace. Hammarskjöld died in a plane crash in Zimbabwe while seeking to negotiate peace between United Nations and Katanga forces. This commitment to unity of those with differences and to peace has become part of our culture, part of our DNA at Saint Paul's. When you cross our threshold this is what you find.

There is nothing self-congratulatory in this. Rather, in a world that is dangerous, where difference is often met by violence, it is our particular witness to turn toward unity and peace. Jesus gives us each other and sends us out to be agents for this mending of creation. We are to invite others to join us. Invite them over the threshold. Note the warning advisory: we are about to be changed. The world is about to be changed. We have met the risen Christ, wounded and glorified, and it has made all the difference.

Amen.

Notes:

1. Kimberly, John R. and Bouchikhi, Hamid, *The Soul of the Corporation: How to Manage the Identity of your Company,* Upper Saddle River: Wharton School Publishing, 2008. Behind this sermon was a preview of his book that John Kimberly shared with me.

Acts 26: 9-21
Galatians 1: 11-24
Matthew 10: 16-22

"The Transition Game"

The Last Sunday after the Epiphany/February 3, 2008

"You will do well to be attentive to this as to a lamp shining in a dark place, until the day dawns and the morning star rises in your hearts."—*2nd Peter 1: 19*

Two years ago I began my ministry among us all at Saint Paul's. We're celebrating a little anniversary today. Two years is not a very long time, but for some reason this anniversary feels like an important transition to me. Transition feelings are ones of being alive, energized, a bit unsettled, not knowing for sure what lies ahead, a mixture of fear and (as one scholar said) confident wandering;[1.] we feel vulnerable, alert, bold and spirited. These are the feelings.

Transition happens when one piece of work is done and another lies ahead. In the Exodus story deliverance from captivity was accomplished. In beautiful imagery, God bore the Hebrews on eagles' wings and brought (them) to himself" (Ex. 19:4). The promised land lay ahead. It was a time of transition. For 2nd Peter, it is a transition from "star to star." The first star appearing in the east guided the magi to the Christ child. A second star, a morning star rising in people's hearts, will mark the occasion of Christ's second coming when all will collectively shout for joy. We are in a transition from one to the other. Jesus' transfiguration on Mount Tabor marks the completion of his work of healing and teaching, and the unsettling turn toward Jerusalem, the place of destiny, of the cross and resurrection.

The reason it feels like a transition to me here at Saint Paul's is that we too have accomplished a great piece of work together in the last two years. Honestly, there was some pain here when I arrived that for many felt unmanageable and we have been able to bear it together. Last year we had the first increase in attendance in five years. This year parish giving climbed ten percent over budget. We celebrated together 150 years of parish history with many, significant and fun events that instead of costing the church money actually earned over $1000 for our Restoration Campaign. The Restoration Campaign has seen to new lighting, new furnaces, a new roof on Dixon House and roofing repairs to the rest of the church. Coming up are a new driveway and safer walkways, handicap access, renovated church school wing, and restored stained glass windows. We are about to begin a second phase with a parish planning process in the spring. In the last two years we identified our parish vision as one of "turning—each to the other—in Christ." We have taken significant steps in outreach especially in our ministry with the homeless. We invited Samaritan Counseling to move its headquarters to our church. We renewed our parish connection to the Sioux Tribe in the Dakotas. Now, like the Hebrews, the disciples and the early church, it feels like we are transitioning into a new phase.

What is expected of us, how do we live, in times of transition? That is a question that has been on my mind. Women's and men's basketball has what is called a transition game. It is an up-tempo game that is played between the half-courts. Transition offense takes the ball from the defensive end of the court to the offensive. What is critical to this part of the game is passing. It moves the ball quickly and opens up a good shot. Transition defense means getting back in position quickly and stopping the ball. What is key to this part of the game is communication. Because the transition game is fast, it has to be played with purpose. A random running team gets careless, takes wild shots and loses the ball. So, transition means getting everyone involved. Communication is fundamental, and the movement is purposeful, not random.

The scriptures today describe how God's people live in transition. The experience of Israel awaiting Moses' return from Sinai, is all involving. The ball, figuratively speaking, gets passed to everyone. God has brought them all out of slavery in Egypt. In thankful response all the people will accept the commandments given on tablets of stone. A time of transition involves everyone. The story of Jesus' transfiguration is also a story of communication. Peter is talking when he should be listening. Suddenly a voice interrupts him. In stunned silence he hears: "This is my Son, the Beloved; with him I am well pleased; listen to him." At a time of transition, communication is very important. When the feeling is one of being unsettled, vulnerable, confident and at the same time afraid, Jesus communicates: "Get up and do not be afraid." Those words "get up" resonate with the Son of Man's being raised up from the dead. It is all part of the promise that is being communicated in a time of transition. Finally, living in transition is purposeful. There is nothing random to it. We are not talking about cleverly devised myths, as 2nd Peter warns. Instead, we have the guidance of eye witnesses, inspired men and women, and scripture. These give purpose and direction to our lives when lived in transition.

We all live with transition. There is transition in the workplace. We change jobs, or the economy shifts warranting a change in how our current work is carried out. There is transition in the home when a baby is born, a child goes off to school for the first time, or young adults set out from home to live on their own. Much of life, like basketball, is playing a transition game. We manage transition best when we pass the ball getting everyone involved. We manage transition best when we communicate so that each knows where the other is. And finally in transition we hold to our purpose so that we do not become careless and lose the ball. Transition is where God is calling us to be today. It is an up-tempo life with a God who moves with us and awaits us in each place where we abide until we reach the journey's end where Christ is all in all and we see God face to face.

Amen.

Notes:

1. Käsemann, Ernst, *The Wandering People of God: An Investigation of the Letter to the Hebrews*, translated by Roy A. Harrisville and Irving L. Sandberg; Minneapolis: Augsburg Publishing House, 1984; p. 44f.

Exodus 24: 12-18
2Peter 1: 16-21
Matthew 17: 1-9

"New Directions—
Finding the Way Forward"

The Fifth Sunday of Easter/April 20, 2008

"Do not let your hearts be troubled. Believe in God, believe also in me."—John 14:1

Jesus declares in a dark world where the beaten path too often leads in the direction of greed—"I am the way." In a world that often defines us by our failure when we fall short, Jesus declares: "I am the way." In a world rent by conflict, the broken Jesus made whole and resurrected declares, "I am the way." Jesus assures, "Do not let your hearts be troubled," when the values of the world and faith collide. "Believe in God, believe also in me." Do not let your hearts be troubled when your fallibility is all too present, and even your faith community falls short. "Believe in God," Jesus said. "Believe also in me." And when we feel alone, Jesus says, we're not. "Believe in God, believe also in me." Life is so much picking our way, picking ourselves up, being picked up by a caring God, growing, redeveloping, renewing, following Jesus, the one who in all things has gone before.

Thomas quite rightly says to Jesus, "Lord, we do not know where you are going. How can we know the way?" The point of change is that the outcomes or by-products are unclear. Life for so many of us is about transition. How can we know the way? Jesus said, "Look at me. I am the way." When we look at Jesus, I mean really look at Jesus in the passages this morning there are at least three things that strike me: forgiveness, belonging to God and prayer.

Stephen learned from Jesus how to live and how to die. His last words were ones of forgiveness. "Lord, do not hold this sin against them." He refuses to allow any final separation to occur between himself and his enemies. There would be no barrier of hatred. I recently read a book by a psychiatrist on the Truth and Reconciliation Commission in South Africa. She wrote that "it is within the grasp of ordinary people to forgive evil and to end generational cycles of violence." [1] Forgiveness opens up a way for healing and transformation. "I am the way," Jesus said.

The Jewish Passover begins today. I hear an echo of the Passover in the lesson from First Peter. The Passover verse in Exodus goes: "And when your children ask you, 'What do you mean by this observance?'" I can hear First Peter's answer: "Once we were no people, but now we are God's people. Once we were broken, but now we are whole. Once we were divided. Now we are community. Once we had not received mercy, but now we have received mercy.

And we will say to our children, 'Once we were not a people, but now we are God's people." The preciousness of each one of us, and yes, each one of us is precious, comes from the fact that we belong to God. God of infinite majesty who needs nothing, desires each one of us as one would a small precious stone. Our spiritual community is made up of these living stones. Oh sure we need to re-point the actual stones of this church, and it will cost over a million dollars. But that is nothing compared to the preciousness of each one of us in God's sight.

The final quality that I can see in Jesus as the way is prayer. From first to last Jesus was a person of prayer. Stephen learned it from Jesus. At the end Stephen also prayed. Saint Augustine once said, "If Stephen had not prayed, the Church would not have had Paul." [2] Paul at this time known as Saul stood by approvingly with the coats of the executioners at his feet. He heard Stephen's prayer and it prepared him, broke open his heart, for the encounter with the risen Christ on the road to Damascus. Prayer reaches out in ways that we cannot foresee to bring all "within the reach of Christ's saving embrace." Jesus is the way of forgiveness, belonging and prayer.

How do we find our way in the midst of change and transition? It is bewildering. Like Thomas, we ask: "How can we know the way?" One of the most helpful analogies to me of making our way in transition comes from Abraham Lincoln as he contemplated the challenges of reconstruction after the Civil War. He said, "The pilots on our Western rivers steer from *point to point* as they call it—setting the course of the boat no farther than they can see; and that is all I propose to myself in this great problem." [3.] Jesus says he is "the way, and the truth, and the life." I like to think that life happens when we direct our way, that is steer toward a true bearing from point to point.

The way starts wherever we stand. Where do we see Jesus? Let us set our course no farther than that. Where do we discern before us forgiveness, belonging and prayer or communion? We take our true bearings on those. Cardinal Medeiros of Boston once said, "Christ comes into my office every day. Sometimes in deep disguise." Can we take time to reflect in our busy lives where Christ's presence is making itself known? There are those who call forth from us forgiveness and prayer, and those whom we did not choose but God did to be our sisters and brothers in Christ. As we work to grow our parish as God wants it to grow, we start where we stand. As far as I can see I can identify for us at Saint Paul's a point of generosity—a generous mission of service, a generous permission to try new things, a generous renewal. This is the point, on this leg of the journey, toward which we steer. Jesus said, "I am the way." I heard a young woman in her twenties on Friday talk of how lost she had become in her addiction to drugs. By the age of 19 she tested HIV positive. What changed her life was coming to the point of realization that despite all she had done, she was still precious to God. She found a caring, prayerful community and experienced personally the power of forgiveness. "Do not let your hearts be troubled," Jesus said. "Believe in God, believe also in me." We don't have to take the whole journey at once, but from point to point as far as we can see, we follow Jesus, who is "the way, and the truth, and the life."

Amen.

Notes:

1. Gobodo-Madikizela, Pumla; *A Human being Died That Night: A South African Woman Confronts the Legacy of Apartheid;* Mariner Books, 2004; p. 118.

2. Coggan, Donald, *The Prayers of the New Testament,* New York: Harper & Row, Publishers, 1967; p. 80.

3. Donald, David Herbert; *Lincoln;* New York: Simon & Schuster, 1995; p. 15.

Acts 7: 55-60
1Peter 2: 2-10
John 14: 1-14

"Foundational Difference-Making"

The Third Sunday after Pentecost/June 1, 2008

"The rain fell, the floods came, and the winds blew and beat on that house, but it did not fall, because it had been founded on rock."—Matthew 7: 25

"That house . . . did not fall, because it had been founded on rock," Jesus taught in his parable. It raises for me the question of what are the foundational things worth paying attention to and preserving. I think of the families who lived at the church for six weeks this spring. They were without homes. I wondered, if I did not have a home and had to travel from place to place until I was helped to find one, what would be the things worth preserving that I would take with me? The question came up again in another form when I considered the Phoenix Lander on the planet Mars. On Thursday it successfully lifted its robotic arm. The purpose of the arm is to dig beneath the surface of the planet to see if the ground might once have been warm and wet and capable of producing life. What would be worth discovering were we to probe the face of the earth, that is, to scratch beneath the surface? What would be worth finding and preserving for others, were we to dig beneath the surface of our lives?

Noah's flood in the Book of Genesis is a story whose purpose is to raise similar questions. It is not a question of whether there really was such a deluge, that is hardly the point. At issue is what is worth preserving and passing on, what are the foundational things necessary to creating a stronger world? The scriptures for this morning tell us that among things worth preserving are: peace, community and an active faith. And because today is our celebration of Rick Alexander's 38-year legacy of music at Saint Paul's, it is worth noting how music weaves together these qualities in our spiritual lives. It helps us discover them and notes how they are well worth preserving—peace, community and an active faith.

Peace. It is not as though the people before the flood were any more violent than we are. This century and the last in fact make them look rather tame. As Paul says, all have fallen "short of the glory of God." What is really worth preserving is a world of peace, not one "filled with violence." Peace is a state of well being not at the expense of others, but the well being of all that is the will of God. Since God is one, when we scratch beneath the surface, all have this inherent quality of belonging that we know as peace. The purpose of music in worship is to inscribe this word of God on people's hearts. It is to flood us with desire for renewal. Each one belongs, each has a place. When I first came to Saint Paul's, Rick commented, "You know, we both try to do the same thing—you in preaching and me in music—and that is to create "magic." We both try to weave a pattern of access in sound and imagination to the Mystery without which there could be nothing, and in which there is peace. This is the power of God for salvation, Paul says. That is, for freedom and relationship.

Community is well worth preserving. In Noah's story, when the earth was dry, everything that moved on the earth went out from the ark in families. Were we to probe the earth with an arm to dig beneath the surface, we would discover something essential in the nature of community. The alternative to our fragmented life-style is the freedom to be in relationship. Music in worship invites a transcendence of the barriers that separate us from one another. When I was in Israel and the West Bank this spring, what I wanted to bring home was the music. Music has a way of crossing fences. Its native speech is community.

A third thing that is foundational for our lives is an active faith. Noah's blueprint for creating an ark is described in great detail. Only one thing is missing—a rudder. There is no way for Noah to steer this ship. He must chart his way by faith. There is nothing complacent about this faith. Rather it entails hard work, planning, a nightmare of management, but above all: trust. This active faith undercuts the suspicion and cynicism that are so much on the surface of discourse. This surface discourse is like the sand that provides no foundation against even a stumbling wind. The wind is a character in Jesus' parable. We miss this in the English translation. There the wind "beats on" the house built upon rock, and it does not crack. The Greek word for "beats on" has the connotation of falling down before in worship. The wind has met its match. It falls down in obedience before an active faith. In translation, the wind "beats against" the house built on sand. In Greek this has the connotation of stumbling. Here the meaning is almost comic. Apart from an active faith one is left with a foundation so weak that even a tripping, doddering wind causes its collapse. In music there is at times a ground bass that anchors the melody. Music too involves an active faith. All music is a movement and a becoming. It does not stand still. We participate in what it will be and in the process become transformed. Growth and transformation are not things over which we have perfect control. They require an active faith.

I like to say that when we give to Saint Paul's, we are making a foundational difference. We are digging deep to things that matter, and upon which everything else rests. The flood story asks, if everything were to be destroyed, what would be worth carrying forward? Our outreach to homeless families poses the question, if we ourselves had no home and had to take our possessions with us, what would be the things worth taking? Perhaps these stories do not touch us and we have never had to choose what is worth preserving; then surely we will all have to choose what is worth leaving behind. Are we satisfied with a world of violence, fragmentation and cynicism, or do we want to assure the remainder of peace, community and an active faith. These are difference-makers at a deep, foundational level. At worship we sing of them, and by doing so, are changed by them. The Spirit that stands within us is made strong; the Mystery that upholds us is so secure, that life's substantial trials like tearing tempests are stilled and succumb to the One whose authority even the winds and the water obey (Matthew 8: 27).

Amen.

Notes:

Genesis 6: 9-22; 7: 24; 8: 14-19
Romans 1: 16-17; 3: 22b-31
Matthew 7: 21-29

"Outpouring—Pouring Out Life Cycle"

The Day of Pentecost/May 11, 2008

"In the last days it will be, God declares, that I will pour out my Spirit upon all flesh, and your sons and your daughters shall prophecy. . . ."—Acts 2: 17

"All of them were filled with the Holy Spirit," Luke says; and then quotes the prophet Joel that God positively poured the Holy Spirit upon all, poured out the Holy Spirit upon sons and daughters and even upon slaves at the bottom of society both men and women. No one is exempt from this pouring out of the Spirit. Our experience of God is an experience of abundance.

Pentecost which we celebrate this morning means "the fiftieth day." Fifty days ago we celebrated Easter after which I was in Israel/Palestine. The State of Israel celebrated its 60th anniversary this week. In 1949 Christians made up 21% of the Palestinians who were permitted to reside in Israel. That percentage today is 9%. Palestinian Christians have been moving out because of long standing prejudice against Arabs. It is called a silent transfer. Nevertheless, Palestinian Christians view themselves as descendants of those who in the upper room over two thousand years ago experienced the outpouring of the Holy Spirit. Their forbearers were the eleven disciples together with certain women, including Mary the mother of Jesus and Jesus' brothers. On this Mothers' Day it bears noting that Jesus' mother was in Jerusalem in that upper room with the others. Mothers, daughters, sons, fathers, those who experience discrimination and those who are free of it—all are filled with the Spirit.

Paul's experience was that the Spirit's outpouring enlarges us through the bestowing of gifts—wisdom, knowledge, faith, healing, the working of signs that point to God, the prophetic call for justice, the discernment of who is guided by the Holy Spirit and who is not, and last of all (what

Paul considers the least of the gifts, though it was one that Paul possessed) glossalalia or the speaking in tongues and the gift of interpreting such speech. Paul uses this list as representative of many more gifts that the Spirit allots to each of us "individually just as the Spirit chooses." Everything we have and everything we are, has been a gift to us. Creation, the air we breathe, the families who nurtured us—we didn't choose any of it. It is nothing we earned nor is it a reward for some achievement on our part. It is all a gift from God and from those who love us.

We are allotted gifts by God in order to give them to one another for the common good. I like to call this the "outpouring—pouring out life cycle." First there is this abundant outpouring of the Spirit from God. No one is exempt. We are enlarged and continually renewed by this outpouring Spirit. We have each been gifted by the Spirit in a unique and wonderful way. We have only to receive it. God has poured it on. Then our response is to pour out what gifts we have, to the community and others.

We find life when we begin to pour out what we have been given by the Spirit. We become fulfilled. Giving changes our lives for the better. That's why I call it an outpouring-pouring out life cycle. It is life-giving. People do not come to church to preserve an institution, as helpful as that might be. No, they are looking for purpose, significance and eternal life. This happens when we experience the outpouring of God's Spirit, the abundance of God's bounty, Jesus' peace. Then we offer our own pouring out of what has been given us for the common good, for the well being of all. That's God's will and in it we find life. This giving is meaning-making for us. We often call it stewardship.

Sometimes when God pours out abundantly, we see scarcity. We see ourselves alone without enough instead of in community with more than enough. Rather than become enlarged we shrivel. Rather than become new we have simply grown old. We retreat to become less than we are. This is where we find Jesus' followers, both men and women. They are huddled behind locked doors, afraid. When we doubt the overflow of the Spirit we behave in ways that are contrary to life. We start worrying and holding on. We stockpile and get protective of what we have. We live with the anxiety of erratic fluctuations in the market. We worry about what we might lose, rather than the life we might gain.

Jesus' antidote to this is his declaration of peace, "Peace be with you." He is not merely greeting his followers or wishing them well. He is stating a fact. God's peace is with you. That poured out bounty and well being is surrounding you right now. Then watch what happens—the disciples' fear is replaced by joy. When we experience the outpouring of the Spirit, feelings of scarcity are transformed to ones of abundance. Worry gives way to serenity. We find life characterized by joy and fulfillment. This cycle of God's giving and our giving is a life cycle.

At Saint Paul's we are interested in getting more and more into that cycle of life. We have received so many blessings. The Holy Spirit has filled us all. We want to grow into a more generous community, one with a generous mission of service, a generous permission to try new things, to enlarge ourselves and to be a place of generous renewal. As Paul suggested we did not receive the Spirit to fall back into a fear of scarcity but to make meaning and find a life that is expansive. When I asked the question what does Saint Paul's mean to you, one person said Saint Paul's was a place to contribute and stretch. Another said I have received such an outpouring of compassion in a time of need I may never be able to repay that love. And that's ok. It is a part of our life cycle. Another said we are a congregation that feeds each other and sends each other out into the world to serve. We receive a bounteous outpouring from God and pour out the overflow of what we have been given, for the well being of all. It's simple stewardship. It is a cycle of life that began all those years ago in an upper room where the Spirit fired up people's hearts and loosened up their tongues to give in word and deed for the common good. And in so doing they found life.

Amen.

Notes:

Acts 2: 1-21
1Corinthians 12: 3b-13
John 20: 19-23

2008

"Overcoming Fear, Seeking Peace"

The Epiphany/January 6, 2008

"In the time of King Herod, after Jesus was born in Bethlehem of Judea, wise men from the East came to Jerusalem, asking, 'Where is the child who has been born king of the Jews? For we observed his star at its rising and have come to pay him homage.'"—Matthew 2: 1-2

It is the twelfth day of Christmas, and your true love may send you 12 drummers drumming, but more likely he or she will say something about dismantling the tree and putting away the ornaments in their cardboard boxes and taking them up to the attic. We celebrate the twelfth day of Christmas as the Epiphany, the appearing of Christ to all the world. The Jewish custom begins the day at sundown, so the counting begins on the evening of December 25th and ends 12 days later on the morning of January 6th or the Epiphany. Today, the Epiphany gospel sends us, rather than drummers, three magi, two kings—Herod and Jesus, and all the chief priests and scribes. Three are seekers, many do not seek at all, and one out of fear imperils Joseph's young, vulnerable family and others as well in the village of Bethlehem.

We begin with those who do not seek at all. The chief priests and scribes can quote the prophet Micah that from Bethlehem is to "come a ruler who is to shepherd my people Israel." But they do not seek that ruler. Not one of them goes to Bethlehem. If we believe the messiah will be a great ruler to unseat Herod and Rome, then that is what we will see or not, and we will miss the true king of deep peace who is the child in Bethlehem. Psychology calls this a "confirmation bias." We tend to see those things that confirm our view of reality, and miss or are blind to those that do not. The chief priests and scribes cannot see what is totally unexpected. Like them we tend to see what we believe.

In addition to confirmation bias, in our modern age the heated up daily demands of fast-paced life cause us to narrow our field of vision. It is hard to see beyond the next deadline. We have lost a sense of Sabbath or sacred rest from phones and faxes and tasks that are never complete. We have tunnel vision, attending to the small but missing the significant. That noted "wiseman" Yogi Berra suggests an alternative—"You can observe a lot by watching." Jesus said you can find a lot by seeking. But it takes a wide, unbiased ability to see.

Secondly, we are sent another in King Herod who actually does see and is frightened. The magi ask to be taken to the king of the Jews. This is the only place apart from the title on the board nailed to Jesus' cross where he is called king of the Jews. Herod is threatened by this potential rival. "Frightened" in Greek means literally "to shake, to stir up and throw into turmoil." This describes Herod and all of Jerusalem with him. From beginning to end peril follows Jesus from those who are threatened by his rule of peace and freedom.

I wonder about the role that fear plays in our world today. Our most primitive, instinctive reaction to fear is either to flee or fight. We see fishermen fearing for their livelihood and who over fish the seas. They know it. They know the fish won't be there in the future. They flee that reality, but what else is there to do? I wonder whether we fear living with limits and so deplete the earth's resources? Again, we flee the facing of consequence. We fear competition and so attempt to remove our rivals. We gear up for the fight. We fear challenges to our way of life. Benazir Bhutto was killed in Pakistan by those who were afraid of a contrasting perspective. In the Northwest Frontier Province of the country news of her death was met by cheers and rifle shots in the air in celebration. An Islamist politician went out to the crowd and reminded them that Benazir was a Muslim too and faithful to her country. Though he and the crowd disagreed with her, he said, her death was a sad day for Pakistan. The politician then led the quieted crowd in prayer. Epiphany asks us to rise above our most primitive instincts. Epiphany asks us to rise above our fears—to begin to seek something else.

The magi are seekers. They are foreign to Judea. It is one of the ironies of the story that foreigners come to seek Jesus, not the residents of Jerusalem. The magi don't share the confirmation bias of the scribes. They signal a wisdom of observation and openness. It seems to me that we too are becoming a nation of seekers. It may reflect our anxiety at overwork and economic unrest. We are looking for something more. The pursuit of happiness is part of our country's DNA. We tend to seek it, however, in fashion model looks or personal careers. That may also be part of our cultural DNA. What yields happiness, however, has much more to do with relationship. For the Christian, it is our union with God and one another in Christ. When the magi enter the house there is this realigning of relationship. The magi are aristocrats who acknowledge a child. They are the rich who pay homage to an ordinary Judean family. They have become members of the same body, sharers in the same promise. As the Letter to the Ephesians says, this is the mystery, wisdom and purpose of God.

When Matthew uses the word "house," as when the magi enter the house, he wants us to think as well of the house church where the Christians of his time worshiped. There, people of different classes and wealth, races and genders, gathered to seek and remember, to celebrate and watch the mystery of salvation unfold in Jesus. Just as we do today. Epiphany, the twelfth day of Christmas sends us not drummers but seekers, and it sends us out as seekers. Magi and members of the body of Christ, we seek not the expected—good looks and career, power and position. We seek what we do not expect—the oneness of all that is in God. This is the source of deep peace. This is the freedom to be who we most truly are. Jesus is king of a mended world. When we discover this, like the magi, we are "overwhelmed with joy."

Amen.

Notes:

Isaiah 60: 1-6
Ephesians 3: 1-12
Matthew 2: 1-12

"Eye Openers—Seeing Beyond Difference"

The Sixth Sunday after Pentecost/June 22, 2008

"But Sarah saw the son of Hagar the Egyptian, whom she had borne to Abraham, playing with her son Isaac."—Genesis 21: 9

"Sarah saw the son of Hagar . . . playing with her son Isaac." This fairly innocuous sentence contains a pun that in Sarah's eyes is disturbing. Hagar's son Ishmael is "playing" with Isaac whose name means "play" or laugh. The image in Sarah's mind is that Ishmael is "Isaac-ing." She feels the chilling threat of Ishmael intruding upon the blessing and promise that is due Isaac, her child with Abraham. The background as you may know is that when Sarah despaired of ever having a child, she gave her Egyptian slave Hagar to Abraham so God's promise to make of him a great nation might be fulfilled. Abraham had a child with Hagar whose name was Ishmael. Later when Sarah had a child of her own, she was deeply troubled that Ishmael might inherit the blessing and promise along with Isaac. So she has Abraham cast out both Hagar and their son Ishmael into the wilderness. This strife over blessing is a generational cycle that perpetuates itself. Isaac's wife Rebekah would give birth to twins, Esau and Jacob. Together with Jacob she schemes to deprive Esau of his father's blessing. This divisiveness and strife continues to this day between young and old, male and female, Black and White, Jew and Gentile, Palestinian and Israeli, to name unfortunately just a few.

Some today describe this either-or world-view as a "dual polarity paradigm." It is either Ishmael or Isaac; it is either Esau or Jacob—and to choose for one is to choose against the other. It is either Palestinian or Israeli; in our country, often, it is either Black or White—and to chose for one is to choose against the other. Paul calls this sin. For Paul sin is not so much an offense as it is a power. It is a dual polarity paradigm, if you will, that holds power over us. It is a life driven by death or the fear of death. We say, it is either them or us. This is the dark humor of the two men being charged by a bear. The one is putting on sneakers. The other exclaims "What are you doing? You'll never outrun that bear." To which he replies coolly, "I don't have to. I just have to outrun you." When we live out of a fear of death we just have to outdo the other person. This perhaps is what explains so much of life's drivenness. The power of sin sets one against the other. It is a blindness. We are blinded by cares and worry. Busy-ness and self-importance are blindnesses. We can't see past any of them. Sin is blind to empathy and God's will for the well being of all.

In contrast to the power of sin that causes such blindness, God works to open our eyes. Hagar and her son Ishmael have lost everything. Alone in the wilderness with no water they await death. Hagar poignantly sits a good way off from her son because she cannot bear to see him die. This is not division or dual polarity but love. Then an angel of God tells her, "Do not be afraid." And God opens her eyes to see a well of life-giving water. Jesus says much the same, "Have no fear . . . nothing is covered up that will not be uncovered" so that you can see it, and make all that is life-giving visible to others. Three times in the passage from Matthew Jesus declares, "Do not be afraid." The gospel writers did not have italics or bold face type to give emphasis, so they used repetition. Matthew wants to emphasize Jesus' assurance, "do not be afraid." Jesus' argument makes me smile. He says, "Don't be afraid." But if you really must fear something, don't worry about what can hurt you physically but can't touch the soul, that core part of you that resonates with God. Instead, fear God who can destroy both soul and body. But then God knows the number of all the hairs on your head and will not let the fall of the least sparrow go unnoticed. So, actually, ultimately, there really is nothing to fear.

We are given eye-opening experiences of God's deep care for each one of us. Jacob who got caught up in sin's power to grasp for himself the blessing of his father, was given an eye-opening vision of a ladder reaching to heaven, just before reconciling with his brother. Our second rector, William Hobart Hare, was describing his missionary work among the Sioux at places like the Standing Rock Reservation where our young people will travel this summer. He said our religion is like Jacob's ladder "whose top, to be sure, reaches into heaven; but only as we enable (people) to see it set up on earth right alongside them, as God placed the ladder alongside Jacob in his vision, will (people) realize that our religion is for each one the gate of heaven." [1] This is not an exclusive sect but a religion in which all are gathered to God. For Bishop Hare there was no dual polarity paradigm. It was not about settler or Indian. The reign of God is a blessing on all. Isaiah prophesied that God's house "shall be called a house of prayer for all peoples" (Isa. 56:7).

The sermon today is about when child's play is no longer child's play, when the creativity and joy of play give way to destruction. Sarah was disturbed by Ishmael's play with Isaac, blinded by the fear that her child might have to share God's blessing. Play gives way to destruction—in our own neighborhood vandals mixed broken glass with sand in the playground of the Germantown Jewish Center. Sin is that power that still holds in thrall those who are threatened by others who are different. Sin sets up a polarity in which the blessing of one diminishes that of another. We counter sin with the power of life, Hagar's well of life-giving water. Don't be afraid to look for it. The power of life is eye-opening. Don't be afraid to point it out. We counter sin by the vision of Jacob's ladder set alongside each that reaches to heaven. Don't be afraid to climb. Don't be afraid to point it out. Don't be afraid to help another step up a next rung of the ladder. God's creative, playful blessing is for all.

Amen.

Notes:

1. Howe, M. A. DeWolfe, *The Life and Labors of Bishop Hare: Apostle to the Sioux;* New York: Sturgis & Walton Company, 1913; p. 337.

Genesis 21: 8-21
Romans 6: 1b-11
Matthew 10: 24-39

"Forgiveness and Singing that will Never Be Done"

The Eighteenth Sunday after Pentecost/September 14, 2008

> *"'Say to Joseph: I beg you, forgive the crime of your brothers and the wrong they did in harming you.' Now therefore please forgive the crime of the servants of the God of your father." Joseph wept when they spoke to him.'*—Genesis 50: 17

Joseph's brothers plead, forgive our crime. Peter asks, "how often should I forgive?" Finally, Jesus (concluding a parable) counsels that we forgive from the heart. Forgiveness is at the heart of Christian community. It is the glue that holds us together. It is so important that there is no limit. At the same time, Jesus remains clear, through the parable he tells, that forgiveness does not exist apart from accountability.

Joseph was asked to forgive a horrendous crime. He was left for dead and sold to slavers by his own brothers. This week we marked the seventh anniversary of 9/11 when planes from Boston, hijacked by terrorists, slammed into the twin towers in New York, the Pentagon in Washington and crashed in a field in Shanksville, Pennsylvania. Nearly three thousand died. What does it mean to forgive in the face of horror. Is Amish forgiveness after the Nickel Mines killing of five school girls, two years ago and closer to home, an exception? Psychologist Pumla Gobodo-Madikizela who served on the Truth and Reconciliation Commission in South Africa wrote, after the horror of apartheid, "But forgiveness does not overlook the deed: it rises above it. 'This is what it means to be human,' it says, 'I cannot and will not return the evil you inflicted on me.' And that is the victim's triumph."[1.]

Forgiveness and rising above the horrendous deed are what Paul means by presenting ourselves as a living sacrifice. It is self-giving, sacrificial living, for-giving that points to the new world that has come in Christ. Don't be conformed to this broken, violent world, Paul says, but be transformed by the renewing of your minds. This is baptismal language. Our whole existence is re-oriented at baptism so that we do not overlook the evil that is in the world but we renounce it, we rise above it. We forgive.

Forgiveness is not without accountability. Jesus follows his saying to Peter to forgive not just seven but seventy-seven times, with a parable the point of which is that we are a mutually forgiving community. The slave who is forgiven by the Lord is accountable to forgive similarly those who are in debt to him. Jesus teaches the same in the Lord's Prayer—"forgive us our trespasses as we forgive those who trespass against us." We are accountable for being a mutually forgiving community.

One may say that forgiveness lifts us into relationship. Without forgiveness we would break apart. Without forgiveness there could be no mending. Forgiveness does not overlook the deed, it rises above it.

Music has a role to play in lifting us above the losses and violence that beset us and our world. Over a century ago the novelist, Willa Cather wrote: "Music first came to us as a religious chant or a love song," and "through all its evolutions it should always express those two cardinal needs of humanity."[2] A religious chant—some see the etymology of the word religious from the Latin re-ligare, to "bind again," and mend. Music helps us rise above what is broken, to find mending and love.

To test this, I went back and looked at the music chosen for September 16, 2001. The choir on that Sunday after 9/11 sang Edgar Bainton's anthem, "And I saw a new heaven and a new earth." Part of the text goes, "And God shall wipe away all tears from your eyes; and there shall be no more death, neither sorrow nor crying, neither shall there be any more pain, for the former things are passed away." Incidentally, on that same day I ended my sermon with similar words taken from the *kontakion* of the burial office: "where sorrow and pain are no more, neither sighing, but life everlasting." The sensibility of both is to raise our eyes above the wrong to where there is mending and love. This is what it means to be human, religious, even triumphant. It is baptismal transformation and renewal. It is the gift of music. It is forgiveness.

Forgiveness rises above wrong done. Music lifts us to that which is mending and loving. Music is forgiveness in song. Let me conclude with a poem written after the end of World War One. With the cessation of violence comes this poem that lifts weary spirits above the horrors of trench warfare. It is a poem of forgiveness entitled, "Everyone Sang."

> Everyone suddenly burst out singing;
> And I was filled with such delight
> As prisoned birds must find in freedom,
> Winging wildly across the white
> Orchards and dark-green fields; on—on—and out of sight.
>
> Everyone's voice was suddenly lifted;
> And beauty came like the setting sun:
> My heart was shaken with tears; and horror
> Drifted away . . . O, but Everyone
> Was a bird; and the song was wordless; the singing will never be done.[3]

Amen.

Notes:

1. Gobodo-Madikizela, *A Human Being Died that Night: A South African Woman Confronts the Legacy of Apartheid,* Boston: Mariner Books, 2004; p. 117.

2. Cather Willa, *The Song of the Lark,* edited with an Introduction and Notes by Sherrill Harbison, New York: Penguin Books, 1999; p. xix.

3. Sassoon, Siegfried, "Everyone Sang," *Picture Show,* New York: E. P. Dutton & Co., 1920.

Genesis 50: 15-21
Romans 14: 1-12
Matthew 18: 21-35

"Lunar Eclipse, Our Masks and God's Grace"

The Third Sunday in Lent/February 24, 2008

"and hope does not disappoint us, because God's love has been poured into our hearts through the Holy Spirit that has been given to us."—Romans 5: 5

"God's love has been poured into our hearts through the Holy Spirit that has been given us." After the Beta Course on Wednesday night I took the dogs for a walk. The skies had cleared. The neighborhood was quiet, and the moon was about a quarter of the way into its eclipse. It looked to me for all the earth as though there was a smudge of ash on the moon. I thought of our being two weeks into Lent, a season that began with the imposition of ashes. The ashen mark on the moon was in fact the shadow of the earth. Psychologists sometimes refer to the broken, stony, dark sides of our personality as the shadow side. We often try to hide them behind a mask of "everything is fine." We present a sunny disposition like the reflected light of the full moon. But despite our efforts, the shadow does not go away—it just comes back later more pronounced than before.

One of the ways that Jesus described sin was this "hiding behind a mask" which is what the Greek word for hypocrisy means. We mask over our mortality and our need for penitence. We try to live without limits and without "having to say you're sorry." Ash Wednesday and Lent are about taking off the masks, attending to them, understanding them, and then keeping in mind both the sunny and shadow sides of who we are—working at becoming more whole, more integrated. It helps that God's love is poured into our whole heart. God lays claim to all of us.

God lays claim to our lack of faith. The Israelites are without water and they are getting pretty testy. Moses asks them, "Why do you test the

Lord?" The people complain their thirst is killing them. Now the irony is (and it's pretty insidious) that the thirstier we are, the less inclined we are to trust that God will provide water. We get testy. The amazing thing is that God lays claim to our whole selves, even that shadow of unfaithfulness we would like to hide.

Christ died for the unworthy, Paul declares. "God proves his love for us in that while we were still sinners Christ died for us." While we still hide behind masks of everything is fine when it is not; of masking over the preciousness of life by thinking we have all the time in the world; of masking over our vulnerabilities or sufferings so that others are shut out—even here God lays claim to us.

In the Gospel, there is a testiness between Jews and Samaritans. The woman says to Jesus, "How is it that you, a Jew, ask a drink of me, a woman of Samaria?" But Jesus does not look at the Samaritan as do other Jews. There is no "holier than thou" mask covering over insecurity. God's love is poured out on both Jew and Samaritan. The disciples get testy when they see Jesus speaking with a strange woman. This was shocking in Jesus' day. Jesus risked being made unclean and excluded from his community. But the disciples all know better than to challenge Jesus' openness by saying "Why are you speaking with her?" In fact, through her conversation with Jesus we can see the Samaritan woman "journey by stages" becoming more whole, more reconciled. She sees Jesus first as a stranger and a Jew, then as a prophet, and finally as Messiah. And all the while she is becoming more whole as God's love is poured into her heart.

Water is the sacrament of God's grace in the scripture we have heard this morning. This water that Jesus gives so refreshes us that distinctions of whatever kind no longer have validity—whether they be distinctions of men and women or religious distinctions between Jew and Samaritan. None are looked down upon as unclean. It's not where you worship that counts but that you worship in spirit and truth. Moses' rock-struck water so refreshes us that we are no longer blind to God's ability to heal and satisfy, no longer testy. Our unfaithfulness is taken up into love. For Paul, God's love is like water that is poured superabundantly into our hearts leaving no corner unworthy of being filled, overflowing.

The Samaritan woman is so full of love, bubbling over with God's grace, she can't help herself. She just has to share it. She doesn't even take the time to pick up her water jar before she heads into town to share the good news. The Gospel of John puts her on the same level as Philip the Evangelist who tells his brother Nathanael to "come and see." Come and see where on the hard, rocky ground of life, God brings forth water. Come and see where even in our unworthiness God pours, absolutely pours, love into our hearts. Come and see the source of spring water gushing up to eternal life. He can't be the messiah, can he? Come and see.

Well, we have come a long way from the ashy shadow on the moon. An eclipse is a good metaphor for those "sunless caverns some of us sink into from time to time," as one explorer of caves suggests.[1] These may be sunless caverns of unfaithfulness, unworthiness or uncleanness. Sometimes they are sunless caverns of loss. I remember a cavernous grief I felt some months after my mother died. One morning I happened to read the 95th Psalm as we did today. And there it said, in God's hand "are the caverns of the earth." God holds all our sunless places. There are no more masks. They are not needed. Because God holds our grief we can look at it and accept it as part of us and find healing. Because God holds our lack of faith we become more believing. "I believe, help my unbelief." Because God holds us, uncleanness is invalidated and all are reconciled. This is the incredible good news. How can we possibly keep it to ourselves? "God's love has been poured into our hearts through the Holy Spirit that has been given us."

Amen.

Notes:

1. Hurd, Barbara, *Entering the Stone: On Caves and Feeling Through the Dark,* Boston: Houghton Mifflin Company, 2003; p. 134.

Exodus 17: 1-7
Romans 5: 1-11
John 4: 5-42

2009

"Transfiguring Vision"

The Last Sunday after the Epiphany/February 22, 2009

"For it is the God who said, 'Let light shine out of darkness,' who has shone in our hearts to give the light of the knowledge of the glory of God in the face of Jesus Christ."—2Corinthians 5: 6

"For it is the God who said, 'Let light shine out of darkness,' who has shone in our hearts . . ." This is the transfiguring vision from Paul that energizes us for whatever lies ahead. God's shining in our hearts is the transfiguring vision that draws us from where we are to all that we can be. It is the transfiguring vision or beacon that acts as a guide pointing out the Way we are to follow. God has shone in our hearts just as "Christ upon the mountain peak stood alone in glory blazing," as we just sang.

There is a movement from the vision of divine brightness to what our eyes and heart perceive that travels at light speed. In between there is the cross, a symbol and reality of suffering and love. The vision, ourselves and the cross weave together a fabric of changed values, attitudes and relationships that the Bible describes as a new earth. God through us, through the transformation of humankind, is trying to save the world by love.

Peter and James and John are led by Jesus up a high mountain. Mountains in the biblical tradition are sacred places of revelation, intimacy and teaching. Something important is about to happen. Jesus' clothes become dazzling white, and he stands with Moses and Elijah, the law and the prophets. Peter gets it, and wants to by-pass the suffering and love of the cross. Let's just build three dwellings now so that God through Jesus, Moses and Elijah may abide fully with God's people. He'd rather avoid the suffering and love part. But, Jesus realizes, that is the only way to save the world.

Elisha knows the energy that will be needed to carry on God's word and work. He is about to be thrust into a position where he cannot know what to expect and yet is to be an instrument of God's saving love. For this, he too needs a vision. He saw a chariot of fire drawn by horses of fire that separated him from Elijah who ascended in a whirlwind into heaven. Elisha in grief tore his clothing in pieces. And then found the double share of spirit to carry on in the divine love that transforms lives.

We can see this vision, suffering and love in our own day again and again in small ways and large. Yesterday there was a memorial service in Buffalo for Beverly Eckert who died in a plane crash a week and a half ago. Her husband Sean had been taken from her in the 9/11 terrorist attack on the twin towers in New York. Whereas Elijah had been taken up in a whirlwind by God, her husband was taken down in a whirlwind of smoke and debris by evil. Beverly would have deeply known Elisha's grief. It was a cross of suffering and love. Two months after the attack Beverly wrote of her phone call with her loved one as he faced death. The language was religious only in the sense that it was deeply loving. "Sometimes pain is part of love," she wrote, "and that is a reality we should be able to accept when we love someone." Sean's words, she said, were "a last, wonderful gift to me, and I treasure them."

Beverly's vision of unconquerable love was a phone call from her beloved from whom she would soon be parted. That last wonderful gift energized her, enlarged her and guided her. What Beverly did shows us today actually how powerful we are even in the face of not just terrorism but mountainous global debt and more schemes to swindle others that seem to be revealed every day. Surely the god of this world has blinded many, as Paul said. But for those whose eyes and hearts are open to vision there is power. Beverly used the transfiguring language of love to work its transformation upon the world. She became a voice for the 9/11 families. She watched protectively over how the new administration would handle terrorism suspects to prevent further attacks. She was a guiding force for a suitable 9/11 memorial. In addition she volunteered for Habitat for Humanity and at a local elementary school.

The time we have to do such things is both enough and never enough. No matter how much time we are given with those whom we love—it is never enough. From his baptism where Jesus heard the words, "You are my Son, the Beloved . . ." to the transfiguration where his disciples heard, "This is my Son, the Beloved; listen to him!" to his death on the cross, Jesus had three years. From her treasured phone call with her beloved, Beverly Eckert was given a little over seven years. But with God nothing good is ever lost. God takes what we have done, in the time we have to do it, and stitches it into the fabric of what will one day be a new heaven and a new earth.

We are all given a vision—it may be of Jesus as it was for Peter and James and John. It may well be the love of another or the loss of one we loved. It may be a moment of beauty, a sense of connection, or an awareness of Providence's shelter. But whatever it is, it is an eye-opening, yes-saying moment. We have more power than we know—the power in some quiet way to mend things, the power to contribute in some way small or large to the well being of others.

Power is not about avoiding the cross, but taking it up in self-giving, even in suffering when it comes, and in love to transform the world.

Today is a visionary time. There is a dazzling brightness for each one of us to see. "For it is the God who said, 'Let light shine out of darkness,' who has shone in our hearts . . ." Let us take hold of this vision today and allow it to enlarge us. Discover the power that each of us has to make a difference. Be astonished at God who can take the simplest and the most complex good that we ever do and weave it into resurrection, the new values of life, the new attitudes of hope, and the new relationships of love that characterize a transformed world.

Amen.

Notes:

2Kings 2: 1-12
2Corinthians 4: 3-6
Mark 9: 2-9

"Righteousness is Relationship"

The Third Sunday of Easter/April 26, 2009

"Little children, let no one deceive you. Everyone who does what is right is righteous, just as he is righteous."—1 John 3: 7

The Letter of 1st John declares: "Everyone who does what is right is righteous, just as Jesus is righteous." This concept of being righteous is a tricky one for us today. If righteousness is having an unblemished moral record either we are masking something about ourselves to uphold this unassailable persona, or we are setting ourselves above the human condition. Paradoxically, if we imagine ourselves greater than human we become less than human.

In some cases righteousness is used to divide people into groups—those who adhere to one set of standards and those who do not. We have staying at our church the Reverend Pervez Baig, a Pakistani priest who has been given asylum in our country. Were he to go back to Pakistan he would be killed. Here at Saint Paul's he is being given sanctuary. I talked with him Friday evening. He spoke of Pakistani Christians processing outside their church as we might do on Palm Sunday being shot in the streets. He is saving the little money he receives to bring his wife and two children from Pakistan to join him in this country. His daughter also would like to be an Anglican priest.

In Pakistan the Taliban have clear standards for who is righteous and who is not. A recent peace agreement gave the Taliban the Swat Valley, a one-time tourist paradise. From there, breaking the treaty, the Taliban took by force the district of Buner. In the Swat Valley they are burning girls' schools, beating and killing officials who oppose their rule, and punishing men and women seen together in public who are unrelated to each other. They would say theirs is a righteous cause.

What does the author of 1st John mean when he says: "Everyone who does what is right is righteous, just as Jesus is righteous?" Does it mean that we are sinless? Then why do we confess our sins every week? Does it mean that we are a group set apart? Actually, it means the very opposite. Righteousness is a relational term.

Righteousness preserves the *new* community in which *all* are given life and esteem by God in Christ. God calls us into relationship with one another. We break this relationship through violence, coercion, diminishment and disregard of others. God's righteousness is the restoration of community through Jesus' self-giving love on the cross. We are to be righteous in the same way that Jesus was righteous, through the costly self-giving love that includes all in community. There can be no true righteousness apart from our fellowship with God. Righteousness means relationship.

What *is* the stuff of righteousness, the glue that holds us all together? First, I think it is a story, a narrative that helps us make sense of things. This story is so beautiful that the only way it can be conveyed is through paradox. "You killed the Author of life," Peter relates, "whom God raised from the dead." Britain's greatest woman hymnist wrote around the year 1800 that in the tomb and left for dead all creation was moving in Jesus. In our Godly Play class the story of Jesus in the tomb tells that it was so quiet you could hear the earth breathe. These stories about Jesus' death and resurrection connect all of life, creation and earth. All is in relationship. It is the righteousness of Jesus. Jesus opened the minds of his disciples and opens our minds to understand the scriptures in this way.

The second aspect of righteousness that holds us in community is forgiveness. Peter declares that in turning to God our sins will be wiped out. The image comes from ancient writing done on papyrus. The ink of that time had no acid and so did not bite into the papyrus. To erase it all that was needed was a wet cloth—the ink simply would wipe away. In the same way God wipes out the sins of each repentant person. 1st John says that Jesus was revealed to take away sins. The resurrection was the long awaited release from exile, from the captivity of sin. In Jesus' righteousness *all* are made righteous. No one is excluded. Righteousness is the loving relationship of humanity with God.

Finally, we are made righteous by faith. It was by faith, Peter said, that the lame man was made strong and able to rejoin the Temple community. It is by faith that we trust in the power of our risen Christ to renew and re-establish our relationship with God and others. It is through faith that we are made righteous, that is we are put in right relationship, by the grace of God. Faith is at the heart of our relationship with God and one another. Without faith our connection is lost.

This is our witness as Christians. God raised the Author of life from the dead. Forgiveness of sins is the consequent new reality for all people. As human creatures we are limited, but the power of God is not. God's love, forgiveness and strength are superabundant. Our witness concerns this power of God for the well being of the world. Jesus in the Gospel of John said, "As the Father sent me, so I send you." We are sent out in the Father's love. In Matthew the risen Christ gave the Great Commission—"Go . . . and make disciples of all nations" not through the power of fear but of forgiveness. Here in Luke Jesus likewise sends us out to proclaim in his Name repentance and forgiveness of sins. Whenever we fall into violent coercion we withdraw from righteousness. Contrary to conquest, beatings and killings to enforce one group's standard of holiness, righteousness is a relationship between God and all people. We are to be righteous as Jesus was righteous—giving ourselves in love for the life of others. We are to bring them into relationship with the Author of life whose compassion is stronger than death, and whose forgiveness was unleashed for all through resurrection. In the Christian context, whenever you hear the word "righteousness" think "relationship." Doing right is about inviting everyone into relationship with the God of the living. And, "Everyone who does what is right," 1st John says, "is righteous, just as Jesus is righteous."

Amen.

Notes:

Acts 3: 12-19
1John 3: 1-7
Luke 24: 36b-48

"Generativity"

The Fourth Sunday after Pentecost/June 28, 2009

> *"For he created all things so that they might exist; the generative forces of the world are wholesome, and there is no destructive poison in them, and the dominion of Hades is not on earth."—Wisdom of Solomon 1: 14*

"The generative forces of the world are wholesome." That phrase we heard this morning from the Wisdom of Solomon is at the heart of any psychologically developed and spiritually mature life. Generative forces within drive us toward wholeness and commit us to loving and working to create a better world for those who come after. "The generative forces of the world are wholesome." We become more generative as we become more mature. It involves our desire to invest the substance of our life in forms of work and ministry that will outlive the self. Generative people want to give something back to society. They want to leave a positive legacy for the future. They are more likely than others to see a redemptive pattern in their lives. Baptism is generative. It seeks a world that is whole, that drives toward unity rather than fragmentation. It rejects evil and trusts in grace. It follows the way of love and peace. Curiosity, courage, perseverance, joy, wonder—I think these values of baptism are the kind of legacy that I would want to leave for my children and my children's children. "The generative forces of the world are wholesome."

I am curious about the generative forces that drive the stories from the Bible that we heard today. What is the legacy the leader of the synagogue might wish to leave behind? How about those who have very little substance like the hemorrhaging woman or the beleaguered Macedonians? When circumstances get out of control, how we handle those circumstances is very much in our control. We can chose to be self-absorbed with little to show for it, or generative and leave a legacy of faith, giving and hope.

The hemorrhaging woman though she has little else leaves a legacy of faith and action. She trusts in Jesus' power to heal. But not just that, she takes action. She grabs hold of the hem of Jesus' garment, and is made well. She does not, like many, duck out on her faith. She faces up and fesses up to Jesus. She worships him and declares what is true. That legacy of faith provides a world of peace. She is generative.

At the other end of the economic scale is the leader of the synagogue. His daughter is at the point of death. No amount of wealth can help him. His world has been thrown upside down. He has some control, however, over how he is going to cope with this. He sets out to find Jesus. And with the proper granting of respect—he kneels down before him—he believes an agreement among honorable people has been made to heal his daughter. Jesus, for his part, delays going to the daughter in order to heal the hemorrhaging woman. The woman departs in peace and word comes that the little girl has died. The delay has resulted in an apparent failure. The story comes to a dead stop. Again, what does the legacy of faith require? Jesus ignored this word of the girl's death, and said to the father, "Do not fear, only believe." Isn't this what we are all asked to do at news of Jesus' death on the cross—"do not fear only believe." The father finds faith and follows. The generative force of life is faith and action.

The "generous undertaking" that Paul mentions to the Corinthians is a collection that is being taken among the Macedonians (who have nothing) for the church in Jerusalem that is in need. Paul does not command the Corinthians to give, but offers this example of generosity from those who have little. He says, and this is important, you can underline it in your Bibles—God does not ask us to give what we don't have, but instead accepts a gift from what we *do* have. We understand God's grace when we give it away, or pay it forward. Jesus proved that on the cross when he gave of himself in love for the life of others. The result of giving is gracious, new life.

Now, we still have that girl who has died. The father, footsteps heavy with grief, continues to follow Jesus to his home where people are weeping and can only laugh at Jesus when he says there is hope. Hope happens when we have come to the end of the line, when there is nothing for it but to turn to God. Jesus takes the little girl by the hand and says, "Little girl, get up!" This is resurrection language—little girl, rise up! And she arises and walks about. Just so we do not lose the comparison to resurrection, the onlookers were overcome with amazement just like the women at the empty tomb when they were told "Do not be alarmed . . . Jesus has been raised . . . But go and tell." Hope and telling of new life are generative, and "the generative forces of the world are wholesome."

We in our community today are no strangers to circumstance that can get out of hand. Like the poor woman who hemorrhaged for twelve years or the wealthy man whose daughter was at death's door, illness can drop the ground right out from under us. The man's wealth was no protection. At the same time poverty does not need to define us. We are not victims. We can take hold of our lives through faith. I was talking with a woman the other day who has overcome two bouts of cancer and is battling a third. Faith is seeing her through. Our giving is also generative. It is a testimony to God's grace. One father left ten percent of his estate to the church. His children did not miss the 3 and 1/3% they would have had otherwise and they were given a lesson of what the father valued that would create a better world. Then there is hope; it is an energy, a little like a coiled spring. I was asked this week to be the speaker at a graduation ceremony for Teen Challenge, a Christian ministry to people whose lives have been thrown out of control by drugs and alcohol. I saw in the graduates how hope had been released in their lives as a positive energy. It is as though Jesus had taken them by the hand and said, "Little girl, get up!" They are all beginning to recognize a redemptive pattern to their lives.

Faith, giving and hope are all generative. They work together to create a better world into which Ethan and Emma may thrive. Baptism is generative. It seeks the kind of world that I want to leave for my children's children. Truly, "the generative forces of the world are wholesome."

Amen.

Notes:

Wisdom of Solomon 1: 13-15; 2: 23-24
2Corinthians 8: 7-15
Mark 5: 21-43

"Setting our Sights on the Father of Lights"

Thanksgiving Day/November 26, 2009

> *Every generous act of giving, with every perfect gift, is from above, coming down from the Father of lights, with whom there is no variation or shadow due to change."—James 1: 17*

"Every generous act of giving, with every perfect gift, is from above . . ." (James 1: 17). This quote from the Letter of James is the heart of Thanksgiving. Thanksgiving is a mindset that looks up to the Father of lights who esteems the world and clothes the lilies. For the Christian, thanksgiving is a whole way of life that includes every day, not just one, because each day brings God's new mercies. At the opposite end of thanksgiving there is negativity. We have all been around negative people. With them we've got to have an exit strategy. Negativity is depleting and is best taken in limited doses. But when we meet up with someone who is thanksgiving we want to stay with that person all day, and bask in the good feelings and positive energy. Wouldn't we like to be around one and not the other? Wouldn't we like to *be* one and not the other? What is it that makes the difference?

Thanksgiving in whatever situation we find ourselves is setting "our minds on the things of the Spirit," to quote Saint Paul. Then, Paul says, we will "live according to the Spirit" (Romans 8: 5). Or, in the Letter of James, thanksgiving is to be a hearer of the word. We hear God has gifted each one of us. God lifts the worry from each one of us. We hear God has brought us to a good land (or at least it could be worse, and that's a mercy), and so we are thanksgiving. We are equally doers of this word. We are grateful, esteeming of others, giving, hopeful. We live out of a mindset oriented to the Spirit. The truth of thanksgiving is that "the view you adopt for yourself profoundly affects the way you lead your life."[1.] If we view ourselves as part of the fellowship of the Holy Spirit we are going to lead a life more oriented toward thanksgiving.

The Scriptures we have heard this morning describe two settings in which we have all found ourselves—the wilderness and the fertile land. The wilderness is a dry place in which nothing seems to grow. Time drags on interminably. We feel pangs of hunger and worry. We have all been there. No one goes into the wilderness unless they really have to, as we teach our children in Godly Play. The other setting is fertile land. We know this place as well. It is a place of bounty. Here, we have gotten what we wanted and more seems within reach. We have wealth (at least relatively speaking) and experience success. The fertile place is where we would all like to be.

Thanksgiving would have us "take care" in the one place and not be "care-worn" in the other. The Book of Deuteronomy describes what it is like for Israel to enter the Promised Land, a fertile place. There is plenty of water and no one thirsts. Everything grows in profusion—wheat and barley, olive and fig trees and pomegranates. There is nothing lacking. Iron and copper are mined from the hills. Here it should be easy to be thanksgiving; but not so fast.

I'm one of those who is always curious to see what verses get dropped from the lectionary. And in this case, right after the description of this fertile land and our blessing the Lord for having given it to us, the very next two words that we don't hear are: "Take care." Apparently the author of Deuteronomy does not want us to be complacent when everything is going well. "Take care." We are warned against arrogance, as though our own power and strength have brought us success. A person who is thanksgiving avoids complacency and arrogance and instead has a mindset that is oriented toward the Spirit. There is humility, gratitude and an approachable joy that are attractive. This is the kind of person we would like to be around. This is the kind of person we would like to *be*. This is what it is like to be thanksgiving in the midst of plenty.

Jesus, on the other hand, spoke to people who were barely making it. Perhaps that is where some of us are. If the word in the midst of bounty is be careful, here it is do not be care-worn. When Jesus in the wilderness says, "Do not worry about your life," he is speaking from experience. After his baptism when driven to desolation, he quotes our passage from Deuteronomy—do not "live by bread alone, but by every word that comes from the mouth of the Lord." Again, it is a question of mindset. If we set our minds on the things of the Spirit we do not have to be care-worn; we can live with thanksgiving, even in the wilderness.

Do not let worries get the best of you, Jesus says. Be in relationship. That's what righteousness really means. Never worry alone. [2] Talk with someone you trust. Make time for friends. Go to church. Pray. Learn to quiet down the critical or worrying inner voice. Hear the word of God's compassionate provision, and trust it. Also be doers of the word. Have a plan of action. Don't let worries get the upper hand. Find out the facts. Try not to lose your sense of humor. I think God chuckles quite a bit. Finally, sing. It is hard to sing and worry at the same time. And, give. Ditto. It is hard to give and worry at the same time. So don't let worries define us. Have a mindset oriented to the Spirit. Wherever you are, be thanksgiving.

We are thanksgiving when we set our sights on the Father of lights. That is where every perfect or compassionate gift comes from. The heavenly Creator is the wellspring of new mercies, and the firm ground of trustworthy provision. Set your minds on the things of the Spirit, Paul says. Raise your sights to the Father of lights. If the choice is between negativity and thanksgiving, choose thanksgiving. You'll be more fun to be around. Actually I know someone who was in the hospital who had plenty of reason to pout but who chose instead to be grateful for small kindnesses, the hard work of nurses, maybe even the food, I'm not sure. Rather than care-worn, he was thanksgiving. [3] He had raised his sights to the Father of lights. And for those of us in a place of bounty, take care not to be complacent or arrogant. When we set our minds on the things of the Spirit there is to be found humility and gratitude. We need to develop this thanksgiving mindset. Be thanksgiving not one day but every day. Let it be a life orientation. Thanksgiving takes place when, as James tells us, we raise our sights to the Father of lights.

Amen.

Notes:

1. Dweck, Carol S., *Mindset: The New Psychology of Success;* New York: Random House, 2006; p. 6.

2. Hallowell, Edward M., M.D., *Connect,* New York: Pantheon Books, 1999. The discussion on worry comes from the document on stress management Hallowell prepared for the Chemistry Department at Harvard, pp. 120-123.

3. Kilgore, Randy, "Humble Reminders" from *Marketplace Moments: A Devotional from Marketplace Network, Inc.,* Volume 2, Issue 20, Sunday, July 6, 2003.

Deuteronomy 8: 1-3, 6-10
James 1: 17-18, 21-27
Matthew 6: 25-33

Global Financial Crisis—triptych

"Wild Fluctuations and Steadfastness"

The Twenty-third Sunday after Pentecost/October 19, 2008

"We always give thanks to God for all of you and mention you in our prayers, constantly remembering before our God and Father your work of faith and labor of love and steadfastness of hope in our Lord Jesus Christ."—*1 Thessalonians 1: 2-3*

I want to speak this morning about the "steadfastness of hope" mentioned in the earliest letter of Paul's that we have, the oldest book in the New Testament, the First Letter to the Thessalonians dictated less than 20 years after Jesus' death on the cross. He writes this letter to new converts in Thessalonica who are anxious about Paul's failure to return to them. Paul warmly replies, I remember your "steadfastness of hope."

"Steadfastness" rings a bell because recent days have been a time of great fluctuation. On Thursday the stock market as measured by the Dow went up and down 75 times in one day. It got me thinking, what do we hold onto that remains fast and secure? It sure isn't the stock market, or the coin of the realm that the Pharisees showed to Jesus.

I remembered a parishioner who loved to play the piano. Her parents raised her on classical music but as a girl she would sneak off to play jazz. She was now an elderly woman. Her health had deteriorated swiftly. Lying in a hospital bed, she had lost her jazzy energy, her ability to walk and even to speak. At the end of the hall was a therapy room in which there was a small, toy keyboard. On one of my visits her husband and I brought it to her and laid it on her lap. Her health had dropped as fast as the market. Would she be able to play this child's toy? What would she play? Unable to talk, but in the notes that followed, we heard: "Jesus loves me this I know for the Bible tells me so. Little ones to him belong. They are weak but he is strong. Yes, Jesus loves me . . ." She communicated in the only way she could her "steadfastness of hope."

Moses had to have something secure in the swift up and down fluctuation of Sinai. No sooner had he gone up the mountain than his people fell down to idolatry. They made the golden calf. Together Moses and God's people were about to journey through a dangerous desert toward a land of promise. The people's idolatry had understandably distanced God. Moses was left anxious about whom they could rely on in the path that lay ahead. God said, "I'll send an angel with you." This did not really reassure Moses. Dissatisfied but not willing to criticize God's choice directly, Moses said (to begin our lesson from Exodus this morning): God, "you have not let me know whom you will send with me." Moses did not want God to remain at Sinai while he and his people had only an angel to fall back on. They needed God. The people needed to know that despite everything they still had God's favor. God partly relents and concedes to go with Moses. This is not enough, Moses replies. How can I be sure I have your favor unless you go with *us,* with me and your people? God agrees, "I will do the very thing that you have asked." Not yet satisfied, Moses asks for a sign from God. "Show me your glory, I pray." To see God's glory does not mean to see God face to face, for no one can do that. It means instead to hear the declaration of God's Name: "The LORD," and to see God's goodness, that is God's grace and mercy that allow God to be with God's people no matter what. This is the steadfastness of hope. No matter how our life falls, no matter the hardship, no matter how we might turn from God, no matter the loss, no matter the illness—"Jesus loves me this I know . . ." Moses is given a sign of constant union not just for himself but for all God's people. Nothing can separate any one of us from the goodness, grace and mercy of God.

If the idolatry of worshiping a golden calf at the foot of Mt. Sinai could not keep God from us, what about the payment of tribute to Rome with coins that bore the title, "Tiberius Caesar, son of the divine Augustus?" Empires like stock markets rise and fall. Hope is what is steadfast, Paul said. The content of our hope comes in the last words of Matthew's Gospel, "I am with you always, to the end of the age." Jesus asks about the image and inscription of the coin. His listeners would have caught a reference to the creation story in Jesus' use of the word likeness or head imaged on the coin. In the Book of Genesis, humankind is created in the image of God, according to God's likeness (1:26). When Jesus asks about the title or inscription on the coin, he likely refers to the Passover story that is inscribed in a phylactery worn by observant Jews on the hand and forehead (Ex. 13:9). Jesus concludes that the things that are the emperor's are those that bear his image. The things that are God's are those that bear God's image, that is all of humankind. All of us as human beings bear God's likeness and inscription. That is our steadfast hope.

The stock market can go up and down 75 times as it did Thursday. Our feelings can swing up and down to the slightest variables—whether the skies are clear or overcast, what we had for lunch, or a comment made in passing at the water cooler. Our spirits can rise up like Moses on Mt. Sinai, and fall as short as the Israelites with their golden calf. We can sell our souls to empire, or acknowledge that our very being belongs to God. But what is certain is that God will go with us wherever our life takes us. Every human being is as much an image of God as Caesar's likeness on a Roman coin. This is our steadfast hope. It is not subject to whim. It is not reversible. Everything can be taken away, even speech itself—but not the song, whether played on a keyboard or the strings of our heart, "Jesus loves me, this I know . . ." There is no hope more steadfast than that.

Amen.

Notes:

Exodus 33: 12-23
1Thessalonians 1: 1-10
Matthew 22: 15-22

"A hand to grasp, a prayer to give"

Fifth Sunday after Epiphany/February 8, 2009

> *"The LORD is the everlasting God ... He does not faint or grow weary ... He gives power to the faint ... Even youths will faint and be weary ... but those who wait for the LORD shall renew their strength, they shall mount up with wings like eagles, they shall run and not be weary, they shall walk and not faint."*—Isaiah 40: 28-31

I was talking with a friend this week. In his career he had served both as a Chief Executive Officer and as a member of the U.S. House of Representatives. We talked about the economic recession, people weary with suffering, some unable to sleep at night. CEOs had not asked hard enough questions about the risks posed by mortgage-backed assets and then the housing price bubble burst.[1] Some people, ordinary people, he said, are not able to cover their borrowings and find themselves silent inside faint with fear. My friend added, "This is an opportunity for the church." This is the time for helping and caring for one another. The church's message is of an everlasting God who gives power to the faint, and lifts up those who hope in the LORD. Now is the time to proclaim this word!

The scriptures give some guidance as to what to make of this opportunity for the church. First, Isaiah and Jesus are keen to know on what we base our value system. We need, they say, a transcendent authority on which to ground our life and our decisions. Without that we place our trust in things that are temporary, that are not strong enough to bear the strains of life or the market. "The LORD is an everlasting God." There is no deceiving ourselves. Even the princes among us, compared to God, are brought to naught. With everyone searching for him, why does Jesus answer it is time to leave and "go on to the neighboring towns?" Peter's household was becoming a brokerage place for Jesus' healing.

All who were sick and possessed gathered at the door. From a temporal point of view for Peter's household there was power to be had. Jesus resists this and leaves. He knew that the only true power, the power that is everlasting, comes from God. That is the kind of transcendent authority upon which we need to base our lives.

Next, Jesus shows us how to act in this time of need. Peter's mother-in-law was faint with fever. Are there those today who are faint with fear? Jesus takes the faint by the hand and raises them up. As in Isaiah, Jesus gives power to the faint. He stands beside the feverish and takes their hand. For our part, like Peter's mother-in-law, weak and in a darkened place, a hand is there, and we take it. That is called faith. God never gives up, God lifts up. We know this by faith. We see it in Jesus.

In addition to taking another by the hand and lifting her up, Jesus prays. Prayer weaves like a thread through the entire Gospel of Mark, beginning, middle and end. The Gospel begins with this prayer after healing; Jesus later withdraws to pray after feeding a crowd of 5000 with 5 loaves of bread. Then at the end of the gospel of course there is Jesus in prayer at Gethsemane. In each case where Jesus is weary or worried, he turns to the LORD in prayer and is given power—power in the end to give of himself in love for the life of the world.

This is the gospel that Paul is obligated to proclaim. God does not give up, even at the cross, but lifts up. God compels Paul to tell this good news to all people of every nation, of various customs and a bewildering array of characteristics. Reach out to everyone. Meet them where they are—princely or poor, trusting in the temporal or in the eternal, feverish or afraid, wearied or worried. Take their hand wherever they might be, but don't leave them there. Paul means to save them, at least some, through service and God's word.

Like Paul, our sacred commission is to reach out in a challenging time to our neighbors of every sort. We might not know if they are hurting. But each one of us needs an outstretched hand. As a church, let's be bold. Help one another and others unfold, like a wing in a thermal, so that together we may rise up as eagles. God's esteem of each creates such an affirming place, where we can be who we are and grow toward the best that God created us to be. As a church let's make crystal clear to all that there is a transcendent authority, or power higher than ourselves, that grounds our every decision. Ours is an everlasting God who puts in perspective our worries, and strengthens us when we weary. And let's follow Jesus by being people of prayer. When there is a need for strength, for courage to face the day ahead, when a soul needs to know they are not alone, then there is an ever present help in God, who is as close as one's breath in prayer. A hand to grasp, an eternal God to trust, a word of good news to give, and a prayer to share—some are surely saved by our boldness in all these things.

Amen.

Notes:

1. *Knowledge@Wharton (Jan 21-Feb. 3) presented the analysis of Jeremy J. Siegel, Russell E. Palmer Professor of Finance at The Wharton School, that "ultimately, the buck stops with corporate CEOs who didn't ask hard enough questions about the risks posed by mortgage-backed assets. He said he and others have wondered why firms like Lehman Brothers, Bear Stearns and Morgan Stanley—which survived the much more severe Great Depression of the 1930s—collapsed during 2008. One reason, he suggested, might be that, back then, these firms were organized as partnerships. In such an organizational structure, the partners would have to risk their own capital. When the partnerships were reorganized as widely held public companies, however, they no longer had such constraints. 'Back when it was a partnership, you had your life invested in that company,' said Siegel, noting that banks also began making higher-return but higher-risk investments in recent years as public ownership increased."*

Isaiah 40: 21-31
1Corinthians 9: 16-23
Mark 1: 29-39

"Dis-lodged and Graced"

The Sunday of the Resurrection: Easter Day/April 12, 2009

"But by the grace of God I am what I am, and his grace toward me has not been in vain. On the contrary, I worked harder than any of them—though it was not I, but the grace of God that is with me."—1 Corinthians 15: 10

"By the grace of God I am what I am," Paul asserts when some of the Christians in Corinth may have questioned his stature. At the heart of Easter is the subject of God's grace. By God's grace Jesus was raised from the dead. By God's grace the risen Christ is a living presence in our lives today. And by God's grace we may allow our experience of Jesus to change our lives.

It is by God's grace that we carry out a mission to the homeless here at Saint Paul's. This past Wednesday in Holy Week as is our custom we gathered to pray for the abandoned poor on the streets and in the shelters of Philadelphia. The numbers of homeless individuals and families are growing. The Director of Bethesda Project and one of their guests named Dennis joined us for worship. Dennis is a musician and artist who has social anxiety disorder and is resistant to staying in shelters. This past winter he went to 30th Street Station for the night where a police officer discouraged him from staying. The officer suggested a café operated by Bethesda Project where he could get free coffee and donuts and watch movies. This sounded impossible to Dennis, but nevertheless, apprehensively, he walked down to the Bethesda Café at 7th and Arch. There, he said, he found such grace, such welcome and acceptance. "By God's grace I am what I am," Paul said. Dennis asks for our prayers because through the Veterans Administration he is in line to move into an apartment of his own.

Now, most of us have not had the experience of being homeless but we all are experiencing the feeling of what it is like to be dis-lodged. We have been dislodged from the usual economic engine upon which we have come to rely for employment, savings, retirement and so forth. Every segment of our society has been dislodged. The church is hit as hard as anyone, though we refuse to give up our mission or our praise. Spiritually, I like to imagine that our depressed economy is on a Sabbath. It has stopped working for a time. It may be a forced Sabbath but nevertheless the economy has come to a rest. Nancy in Lent spoke of Sabbath as the interruption of our endless cycle of acquisition, achievement and anxiety. We come to a stop long enough so that we learn to trust in God's grace.

Sabbath gives us the opportunity to reflect upon how we want to live? When Mary Magdalene encounters the stranger whom she supposes is the gardener but is in fact the risen Christ, Jesus asks her, "Whom are you looking for?" This question parallels an earlier one where Jesus asked of his first disciples: "What are you looking for?" (John 1: 38). With the economy on a Sabbath rest, and with each of us dis-lodged from the mushrooming cycle of acquisition, achievement and anxiety, what and whom are we looking for? Easter proclaims the answer: the grace of God. Resurrection is not something to be acquired or achieved; it is totally an act of God's grace.

What is this grace that we are looking for? Peter in our first lesson today says it is the grace of non-partisanship. "God," he says, "shows no partiality." This is the grace of knowing that we all belong to God. We are not apart from one another, whether Jew or Gentile, homeless or housed, dislodged or secure, rather we are a part of one another in community. When we become divided, then, Paul says, return to that original resurrection energy, the story of grace and forgiveness that is the glue that holds us together. Christ died Paul says for the forgiveness of sins. He was raised by the grace of God on the third day—a day of new creation. This is the grace of new community that was delivered to Paul who hands it on to us.

In addition to the grace of being at one with others there is the grace of being at one with oneself. This is the grace of that profligate, prodigal son in Jesus' parable who ran away from home with his father's possessions and lost them all. He finally came to himself instead of being beside himself. In the end homeless and dislodged, he trusted in one thing, that he could throw himself upon his father's grace. We are justified not by what we can do or not do. It's God's grace that accepts us. "By the grace of God," Paul said, "I am what I am." We may find this grace in a homeless café, in an economy that is not working (that is on Sabbath, so to speak), and in a community in which we know, truly know, that we are not alone.

Finally, there is grace under fire. This is being present where we are, even when where we are is disconcerting. Mary Magdalene is at the tomb while it is still dark. Darkness in the Gospel of John represents an unredeemed world. Mary remains present. In confusion and fear Mary has presence of mind. In sadness and weeping Mary endures. In the presence of angels, disconcerting as they may be, Mary stays. Surprised by a stranger, supposing him to be the gardener, Mary persists. Hearing him call her name, recognizing the risen Jesus, grabbing hold for joy and having to let go, Mary abides. This is grace under fire. It is showing up, being present and trusting in the presence of God.

In a year when we may feel dislodged or know others who do, when we are apprehensive, and the economy is not working, we may take a lesson from a homeless man who discovered the grace of God in an Arch Street café. Paul put it this way when others questioned his stature, "By the grace of God I am what I am." This Easter is a good time to reflect on how we might answer Jesus' questions: "Whom and what are you looking for?" Is it possible to live differently than we did before the economy ceased working and went on its "Sabbath?" And what might that look like? Perhaps we will face up to the limits of what we can achieve on our own. The One who had seemed strange to us before, we may now recognize as the Christ for whom we had been searching all along. In the body of Christ there is community where all belong. In the love of Christ our whole self finds acceptance. In the Spirit of Christ we discover courage to stand under fire and in the face of fear. It is all by God's grace. Christ is Risen—by the grace of God.

Amen.

Notes:

Acts 10: 34-43
1Corinthians 15: 1-11
John 20: 1-18

Epilogue

Seek the Peace of the City

A Meditation
November 24, 2008

I. Introduction

"Seek the peace of the city," wrote Jeremiah to the exiles in Babylon. The exiles, he knew, would be there an indefinite time. It would be best that they seek the city's welfare. One might even say that here is an intimation of Jesus' "love your enemy" (Matt. 5:44). In addition, the exiled, economically dislocated Israelites are to worship and pray to God there. The God of Israel is to be met beyond borders, even beyond the borders of Jerusalem. Seek the peace of the city.

This morning a funeral mass was held at the Cathedral Basilica of Saints Peter and Paul for Sergeant Timothy Simpson who was killed a week earlier. He became the fourth Philadelphia police officer killed in the line of duty this year. His partner had been killed less than seven months ago. Violence against police in our city runs counter to the national trend of a one-fifth decline in officers' deaths in the line of duty. Commissioner Charles H. Ramsey said, "he had never witnessed such a toll on police in his 41 years on the job."[1] While police deaths are up, homicides in the city though still numbering 300 are considerably lower than in previous years. According to Lawrence Sherman of the Jerry Lee Center of Criminology at the University of Pennsylvania, the conditions for violence include the high number of illegal guns on the streets, broken families and concentrations of poverty. Mayor Nutter addressed our Diocese (The Episcopal Diocese of Pennsylvania) on the issue of hand guns and safety. Sociologist Elijah Anderson in his book *Code of the Street* emphasized economic dislocation and the alienation and weakening of the family structure that goes with it as the condition for a street code of violence.

As much as anything the violence in Philadelphia was my motivation to join a Delaware Valley delegation of Jews, Muslims and Christians to visit Israel and the West Bank during this past Easter Week for the purpose of peace-making. Would a journey to the center of the world's most intractable violence provide any insight for seeking peace at home? Upon return we have formed the Interfaith Community for Middle East Peace (ICMEP) in order to bring the faiths together in their capacity to be vehicles of peace.

This year's violence in Israel included the death of Roni Yechiah in a rocket attack at the Israeli town of Sderot on February 27. It was the first death by rocket in nine months. In the fighting that followed over 120 Palestinians and 2 Israeli soldiers were killed. After only a week, on March 6, in retaliation for the Palestinian deaths in Gaza, an Israeli Arab residing in Jerusalem opened fire on the Mercaz Ha Rav Yeshiva leaving eight students dead and eleven wounded. On Easter Monday (March 24), two weeks later, we left for Jerusalem. In the air over the Atlantic I read the final verses of Mark's Gospel appointed for the day: "But go, tell his disciples and Peter that (Jesus) is going ahead of you to Galilee, there you will see him, just as he told you" (Mark 16:7). After the crucifixion of exile, officers killed in the line of duty, hundreds of homicides, rocket attacks and a revenge killing, I was going to see Jesus in whom there is that "peace of God, which surpasses all understanding . . ." (Phil. 4:7).

II. Listening

As a delegation we travelled with the purpose of listening. Our leaders were Maha El-Taji, an Israeli Arab, and Leah Green, the founder and director of the Compassionate Listening Project. Our thesis was that listening with the heart corrals differing experiences, pain from opposing causes, and holds them in a safe environment allowing for the appreciation of one another's common humanity. The process of compassionate listening would create a shift from an attitude of defensiveness or a fixation on woundedness to what is at our heart—our loves, our deep desire for peace, and our empathy for others. The only way to help another get to this heart or core of empathy is for us to be in our own heart. By changing ourselves, by being more heart-ful, we can help another to make their own transformation. This was the idea.

Listening is at the heart of personal justice for Theologian Paul Tillich. In a small book entitled, *Love, Power and Justice,* he wrote, "In order to know what is just in a person-to-person encounter, love listens. It is its first task to listen. No human relation, especially no intimate one, is possible without mutual listening. Reproaches, reactions, defenses may be justified in terms of proportional justice. But perhaps they would prove to be unjust if there were more mutual listening. All things and all (people), so to speak, call on us with small or loud voices. They want us to listen, they want us to understand their intrinsic claims, their justice of being. They want justice from us. But we can give it to them only through the love which listens." [2.]

Rami, a Jew who lost his daughter in a suicide bombing, beset with outrage, was able to utilize that energy creatively by speaking for peace through the Bereaved Parents' Circle. Once when speaking to a Palestinian school, the principal warned the student body, "Don't listen to him. He will make you weak." The message is that a certain hardness is necessary for survival, let alone for fighting for what is right. The contrast is between what Tillich called the reproaches of proportional justice, and the mutual listening of creative justice. It is possible to listen deeply without being less assertive about what one believes to be right.

When listening is unexpectedly practiced at a checkpoint real human interaction and healing take place. There are about eighty checkpoints within the West Bank. Their purpose is to restrict the movement of Palestinians and so thwart terrorist attacks. In addition there are as many as 150 to 200 "flying checkpoints" that are set up for a few hours every day. Army vehicles stop along a road to check all Palestinian vehicles as well as Israeli cars carrying Palestinian residents. B'Tselem (The Israeli Information Center for Human Rights in the Occupied Territories) observes that, "Cases of direct physical violence by soldiers against Palestinians wanting to cross the internal checkpoints have become an almost daily occurrence since the beginning of the second Intifada."

We met with leaders of a Creativity for Peace camp held twice each summer in New Mexico for Israeli and Palestinian girls. After an experience there an Israeli came of age for military service and was a soldier assigned to a checkpoint. One day she noticed a small Palestinian boy waiting and terrified with a paper airplane in his hand. She made herself a paper airplane and together they played for a bit and he began to laugh. On another occasion, a man with severe diabetes came to the check point. He did not have the proper permit. It is hot and as he stands, he is suffering. She gets up and takes her chair and has him sit down while he waits. Her fellow soldiers give her looks and wonder what is wrong with her!?! She is listening to the needs of those who wait in line. In her small way giving them justice.

III. Dialogue

Dialogue or lack of it is seen in contrasting views of a Jewish spokesman for the settlement at Hebron and a Sufi Sheikh in Jerusalem. Hebron is the only Palestinian city on the West Bank (other than East Jerusalem) with an Israeli settlement in its center. B'Tselem explains, "Over the years, the army has created a contiguous strip of land in the city along which the movement of Palestinian vehicles is absolutely forbidden ... At the present time (2007), the only persons allowed to move about freely along this strip are settlers and Israeli security forces. The center of this strip contains many sections of street on which even Palestinian pedestrians are forbidden."

We asked David Wilder, a spokesman for the settlement, if he had any personal relationships with Palestinians. "You can't converse with people who are trying to get you to leave," he responded. "If you let down your guard they'll slit your throat. Israel is at war. The only give-and-take we've seen is 'we give/you take.' People like Bin Laden will do barbarous things to you." When asked what was his greatest disappointment, I was interested to hear him reply that he did not achieve enough. He seemed to me someone very much motivated by achievement. Though achievement is a fine motivation, it can lead some people to view others as obstacles and to be authoritarian as leaders. They may look at situations as a zero sum game—it's either them or us. Compassionate listening provides an alternative to this expression of the achievement motive. Here is Sheikh Abdul Aziz Buchari, the direct descendant of Muhammad ibn Ismail al-Bukhari (810-870). Muhammad al-Bukhari compiled collections of traditions (hadiths) in Sunnite Islam.

Sheikh Buchari said, "The Crusaders' war was carried out under the name of religion. In reality it was not religion but conquering. When people say they are fighting over religion, it's really over power that they are fighting. People are upset today over the dividing wall Israel is building, but the real wall is in our heads. If we want to overcome that separation we need to talk to one another. There are plenty of Muslims and Jews here, but we never talk to each other! Some people say, 'Well, we might talk, but we have to find people in the other group who really want peace—then we'll have something in common. We can't expect to talk with extremists.' But those are precisely the people we need to bring into the talks—extremists from both sides. If we do not include all the people of faith in the peace process, they'll speak out in other, less constructive ways. We need to specifically include the 'extremists.'"

IV. Anger

Rami, referred to earlier under "listening," served with a tank crew in the 1973 Yom Kippur War. All together there were 11 tanks. By the end there were three. Rami lost some good friends. He came back from that war a very angry man. 10 years later Rami now married had a daughter who grew to be a vivacious and lovely girl. Then a few days before Yom Kippur at the start of the Second Intafada in 2000, she with several other children were killed by two suicide bombers. He spent the longest night of his life searching the neighborhoods for her, then the hospitals and finally the morgue. A husk of a man, during the seven days of Jewish mourning one thousand people came through his house. One visitor suggested a group for bereaved parents whose goal was peace, to whom Rami bitterly responded, "How dare you!"

Anger, he discovered, is double-edged. Rami had to decide what he would do with his anger. He began to think that vengeance would not bring back his daughter, another Palestinian death would not cause her return. Anger would just fester and eat away at him from within. Pumla Gobodo-Madikizela in a book about the legacy of apartheid in South Africa writes that, hateful emotions "are a burden that prevent the victim from fully coming to terms with the trauma and moving on." [3.] On the other hand, anger was the energy to lift him above himself, to give his life purpose. He found that by telling his story through the Bereaved Parents'

Circle he could bring awareness, the humanness of both sides, the need for an end to the killing.

At the Creativity for Peace Camp an Israeli girl tells her story of losing two friends in a suicide bombing. It made such a difference to her to tell this story in the presence of the enemy. This is deep, emotional work. The process might start with a paper bag filled with twenty words such as Holocaust, checkpoint, suicide bomber and so on. The girls will write what they feel about those words. Then the fur flies! If a girl can say, "I hate you;" "I don't trust you," then it is possible for her to move toward love. But first there needs to be listening with compassion and authenticity. When there is the breakdown, then there is the possibility for break-through. Dr. Pumla Gobodo-Madikizela in her book, *A Human Being Died That Night,* explains "there are internal psychological dynamics that impel most of us toward forming an empathic connection with another person in pain, that draw us *into* (her) pain, regardless of who that someone is."[4] After the Camp one Palestinian student in university listened as her professor said terrible things about Israelis. She stood up and said, "I have a different experience of Israelis," and she told her story.

After visiting with leaders of the Peace Camp we went to Taghba on the Sea of Galilee which is where the trauma of Peter's three-fold denial is confronted with Jesus' three-fold question, "Do you love me?" (John 21: 15-17) It struck me that here was the same catharsis: breakdown, breakthrough and transformation.

V. Forgiveness

Esther Golan was born in 1923. She escaped the Holocaust with the Kinder Transport. Kinder Transport was a British response to the pogrom of November 9 and 10, 1938 in Germany remembered as Kristallnacht ("Night of Broken Glass"). German and Austrian Nazis burned and destroyed 267 synagogues, killed 100 people, smashed 7,500 Jewish stores (all that remained in the Reich), and incarcerated nearly 30,000 in concentration camps. Sponsored by the British Jewish Refugee Committee, 10,000 children left Germany in sealed trains to find refuge with foster families in homes, or on farms, group homes and orphanages throughout Great Britain Later Esther emigrated to Israel, and we met her at her home in Rehavia, Jerusalem. She says that in her natural family the word "hate" was not allowed. She concludes that, "hate brings hate brings self-hate."

When asked about the Nazis and forgiveness, Esther replied, "Forgiveness can only be given to those who did the harm. The perpetrators in this case are all dead, so there is no forgiveness." There is truth to what Esther says, and it is part of the case I might make against capital punishment. Still I wonder whether it is not possible for the victim to forgive a perpetrator who is no longer present. Pumla Gobodo-Madikizela suggests that perhaps it is. She says forgiveness "is a choice the victim makes to let go of the bitterness." [5] She observes that forgiveness can open up for the victim a new path of healing and conversely not to forgive can mean closing the door to transformation.

Nevertheless, Esther noted the conversations that are currently going on between Israel and Germany. "If we can have conversation with Germans, then why do we not sit down with Palestinians?" The goal is not to ignore our disagreements. Rather, she said, what is necessary is to live under creative tension, to live with difference. Our aim of Compassionate listening is to move toward this experience of dialogue. Dr. Gobodo-Madikizela explains that this dialogue "is critical if victims (of whatever side) are to live again with perpetrators in the same society, or indeed if they are to live in greater harmony with themselves." [6]

VI. Hope

Combatants for Peace is an organization with both Palestinian and Israeli counterparts. They are Palestinians who have served time in Israeli prison and Israeli soldiers. Both have sworn off violence for peace. We spoke with the Palestinian Suleiman al-Hamri. He contrasted big dreams with small hopes. "There's a difference between us and some who work for similar goals. You can either work for the Great Dream or for small hopes. The Palestinians who work for 'the Great Dream'—like Hamas—want to open their eyes one day and see not one Israeli still in the Holy Land. Likewise with Israelis—people like Lieberman (Deputy Prime Minister and Minister of Strategic Affairs in Israel who advocates transferring Israeli Arab citizens to neighboring Arab countries)—their 'Great Dream' is to see the total elimination of all Palestinians. But we have chosen to work for what I call the small hopes: that Israelis and Palestinians will be able to live together in peace, and with mutual respect and understanding. We are ready to cooperate with all people and groups. To get there we are starting to work not only on the military issues we started with, but on social problems, on educational problems as well."

At Wi'am, the Palestinian Conflict Resolution Center in Bethlehem, its Director Zoughbi al-Zoughbi writes: "As a Christian, I am always hopeful . . . Hope is a matter of choice. Hope is not only an emotional thing but also a reasonable approach to fight against hopelessness and frustration, which will lead only to hate. Hope is the nonviolent approach to struggle that will not demonize the other but will *invite* the other to join. Hope is an oasis of interactions of people from different backgrounds and walks of life to see new possibilities. Hope allows people to adopt different approaches to create a healthy atmosphere. Hope is the gift of uplifting the spirits of the people who are paying a heavy price in pain. Hope is to walk with them, to share with them, and of course to help them see the possibility of a different reality. Through the work of Wi'am and through our partners, we see that hope truly soars even in the midst of trauma and injustice."[7]

On the second Sunday of Easter, the Psalm for morning prayer proclaims Suleiman's "small hope": "He has established peace on your borders; he satisfies you with the finest wheat" (147:5).

VII. Encounter

We spent our last night and morning in Israel at Neve Shalom/Wahat al Salam, set up as a joint model village in 1972 by a group of Jewish and Arab Israelis. In the United States studies of Black and White racial identity have shown that the identity of a person of one race is constructed in the significant encounter of oneself through the meaningful engagement with those of the other race. In 1972, a group of Arabs and Jews decided to conduct an ongoing encounter by living together, and so Neve Shalom/Wahat al Salam ("Oasis of Peace") was born. It is a lived response to a history of division.

In 1976, this community formed the School for Peace. The youth encounters alone bring one thousand Jews and Arabs to the School each year.

The School accepts young people aged sixteen and seventeen which is the age when they begin shaping their social and political identities. The School is affiliated with Hebrew University. One wall of the "Clubhouse" is a one way mirror through which, unseen, social psychologists may observe the group processes taking place. The School makes extensive use of Social Identity Theory which has grown from Harvard psychologist Gordon Allport's "contact hypothesis" posited in his classic work, *The Nature of Prejudice*. The aspiration of the School is "to unravel and then reconstruct participants' identities because only an encounter between confident identities can lead to a genuine meeting of equals and permit the option of building a more humane and just society." [8.]

The scripture reading for Tuesday morning before we left captured much of what our delegation had been about in this Easter Week and following. In First Peter 1: 22, I read:

> "Now that you have purified your souls by your obedience to the truth so that you have genuine mutual love, love one another deeply from the heart."

VIII. Conclusion

The experience of violence and peace-making in Israel holds potential lessons for us here in Philadelphia. Certainly in both places there are political and systemic issues to be addressed. In Philadelphia these would include hand guns and public safety, job creation (that pays a living wage), and training.

I was struck by the importance of encounter between people with differences, particularly at the age of adolescence when political and social identity is being shaped. We see this through the sharing by members of the Bereaved Parents' Circle in schools, peace camps and "schools for peace."

There is clearly a spiritual dimension to peace-making, that includes listening with empathy that validates the other person, gives a degree of justice and shifts future behavior; dialogue that risks meeting the other whose position is diametrically opposed to one's own; recognition of the energy of anger for creative difference-making; the transformative power of forgiveness; and the hope that takes small steps and includes people whose differences might otherwise divide them.

IX. Bibliography

Anderson, Elijah, *Code of the Street: Decency, Violence, and the Moral Life of the Inner City,* New York: W. W. Norton & Company, Inc., 1999.

Gobodo-Midikizela, Pumla, *A Human Being Died that Night: A South African Woman Confronts the Legacy of Apartheid,* New York: Houghton Mifflin Company, 2003.

Goldstein, Stephen, *Israel-Palestine: A Mission Study for 2007-2008,* Women's Division, General Board of Global Ministries, The United Methodist Church, 2007.

Halabi, Rabah, Editor, *Israeli and Palestinian Identities in Dialogue: The School for Peace Approach,* New Brunswick: Rutgers University Press, 2004.

Tillich, Paul, *Love, Power and Justice: Ontological Analyses and Ethical Applications,* New York: Oxford University Press, 1954.

Notes:

1. *The Philadelphia Inquirer,* 11/19/08, p. A11.

2. Tillich, Paul, *Love, Power and Justice: Ontological Analyses and Ethical Applications,* New York: Oxford University Press, 1954; p. 84.

3. Gobodo-Midikizela, Pumla, *A Human Being Died that Night: A South African Woman Confronts the Legacy of Apartheid,* New York: Houghton Mifflin Company, 2003; p. 96.

4. *Ibid.,* p. 127.

5. *Ibid.,* p. 97.

6. *Ibid.,* p. 119.

7. Goldstein, Stephen, *Israel-Palestine: A Mission Study for 2007-2008,* Women's Division, General Board of Global Ministries, The United Methodist Church, 2007; p. 162.

8. Halabi, Rabah, Editor, *Israeli and Palestinian Identities in Dialogue: The School for Peace Approach,* New Brunswick: Rutgers University Press, 2004; p. 8.

Edwards Brothers,Inc!
Thorofare, NJ 08086
20 December, 2010
BA2010354